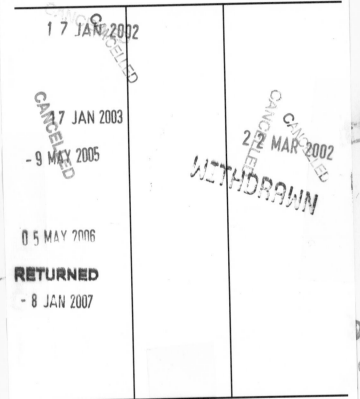

COLLEGE LIBRARY

**Please return this book by the date stamped below
- if recalled, the loan is reduced to 10 days**

1 7 JAN 2002		
7 JAN 2003		2 2 MAR 2002
- 9 MAY 2005		WITHDRAWN
0 5 MAY 2006		
RETURNED		
- 8 JAN 2007		

Fines are payable for late return

Trampolining

for Coaches and Performers

CRPYK

Trampolining

for Coaches and Performers

Rob Walker

A & C Black · London

First published 1988 by
A & C Black (Publishers) Limited
35 Bedford Row, London WC1R 4JH

ISBN 0 7136 5606 9

British Library Cataloguing in Publication Data

Walker, Rob
    Trampolining for coaches and performers.
    1. Trampolining
    I. Title
    796.4'7   GV555
    ISBN 0-7136-5606-9

Printed and bound in Great Britain by
Adlard and Son Limited, Letchworth, Hertfordshire SG6 1JS

Contents

Foreword 9

Acknowledgements 9

Introduction 11

**1 Safety Code for all who Supervise,
Teach or Take Part in Trampolining** 13

The Hall and Equipment 13
Checking the Equipment 13
Folding and Unfolding the Trampoline 14
The Teacher 15
The Performer 15

2 Basic Jumping Skills 16

Arm Action at Take-off 17
Rotation about the Lateral Axis (Initiated by Leaning) 20
Rotation about the Longitudinal Axis (Twisting) 20
Plain Jump 21
Tucked Jump 21
Piked Jump 22
Piked Straddle Jump 22
Straight Jump with Half Twist 22
Straight Jump with Full Twist 23
Seat Drop 24
Seat Drop Half Twist to Feet 25
Half Twist to Seat Drop 25
Swivel Hips 26

Seat Drop, Full Twist to Seat Drop 26
Front Drop (Straight) 27
Front Drop Tucked 29
Front Drop Piked 30
Bouncing on the Back 30
Flat Back Drop from Feet 31
Back Drop (Straight) 31
Back Drop Tucked 32
Back Drop Piked 32
Back Drop from one Leg 33
Half Twist to Front Drop 33
Half Twist to Back Drop 34
Front Drop, Half Twist to Feet 34
Back Drop, Half Twist to Feet 35
Full Twist to Back Drop 36
Full Twist to Front Drop 36
Front Drop, Full Twist to Feet 37
Back Drop, Full Twist to Feet 37
Front Drop to Back Drop 38
Back Drop to Front Drop 38
Cradle (Early Twist) 39
Cradle (Late Twist) 40
Corkscrew (Back Drop, One and a Half Twists Forwards to Back Drop) 40
Turntable 42

3 Introduction to Somersault Rotation (Including Side Somersaults) 43

Hands and Knees Drop, Forward
    Turnover to Back Drop 43
Hands and Knees Drop, Forward
    Turnover Tucked to Seat Drop   43
Tucked Front Somersault to Seat Drop 44
Front Somersault Tucked 45
Front Somersault Piked 46
Front Somersault Straight 47
One and One Quarter Front Somersault
    Tucked 48
Back Pullover Tucked (First Stages) 48
Back Pullover (Bomb Type) 49
Back Pullover to Stomach 50
Back Pullover to Feet with Leg Kick 50
Back Somersault Tucked 51
Back Somersault Piked 52
Back Somersault Straight 52
Back Somersault Tucked to Seat Drop 54
Tucked One and One Quarter Back
    Somersault to Back Drop 54
Side Somersault 55

Hands and Knees Drop, Forward Turnover
    with Support 67
Front Somersault Hand Support 68
Hand Support Behind Neck for Back
    Somersault Preparation 69
Back Somersault with Support 70
Crash Dive Support 71
Half Turn into Three-Quarter Front
    Somersault Support 72
Three-Quarter Back Somersault Support 73
Barani Support 73
Front Somersault with Full Twist Support
    (Hand) 74
Back Somersault with Full Twist Support
    (Hand) 75
Back Somersault with Full Twist in Safety
    Harness 76
Back Kaboom Support 77
Ball Out Support 78
Preparation for the Cody with Hand
    Support: One or Two Persons 79
One and Three-Quarter Front Somersault in
    the Rig 80

4 Support Methods 57

General Principles 57
Use of the Crash Mat 57
Spotters 59
Checking the Rig 59
Using the Rig 60
Kipping 62
Hand Holds for Supporting 63
Front Drop Support 63
Back Drop Support 64
Half Twist to Back Drop with Support 65
Full Twist to Back Drop with Support 65
Back Drop, Half Twist to Feet and Full
    Twist to Feet 66
Support for Back Pullover 66

5 Skills to and from the Back and Stomach with and without Twists 82

Three-Quarter Back Somersault 82
Backward Rotation from the Front Landing
    Position (Cody Kick) 83
Cody 83
Crash Dive, Three-Quarter Front
    Somersault Straight 85
Half Twist into Three-Quarter (Crash Dive)
    Front Somersault 86
Forward Rotation from the Back Landing
    Position (Ball Out Kick) 87
Forward Turnover from Back to Back
    (Porpoise) 88
Ball Out, Tucked from Forward Turnover
    or Crash Dive 88

Ball Out Barani 89
Baby Fliffus, Cradle Back 90
Ball Out Barani Straight 91
Front One and a Quarter Somersault from
    Back with One and a Half Twists (Rudi
    Ball Out) 92
Cat Twist 93
Front Kaboom 94
Back Kaboom 95

6 Somersaults from the Feet with Twists 96

Barani 96
Back Somersault Straight with
    Half Twist 97
Back Somersault with Full Twist 99
Front Somersault with Full Twist 100
Front Somersault with One and a Half
    Twists (Rudolph) 101
Back Somersault with Double Twist 103
Front Somersault with Two and a Half
    Twists (Randolf) 103
Triple Twisting Back Somersault 106

7 Multiple Somersaults 107

One and Three-Quarter Front Somersault
    Tucked 107
One and Three-Quarter Front Somersault
    Piked 108
Double Back Somersault 109
Double Back Somersault Piked 111
Double Back Somersault Straight 112
Two and Three-Quarter Front Somersault
    Tucked 113
Triple Back Somersault Tucked 115

8 Multiple Somersaults with Twists, Fliffes 117

Introduction – The Terminology of
    Multiple Somersaults 117
Barani Out Fliffus Tucked 118
Barani Out Fliffus Piked 119
Barani Out Fliffus Straight 120
Barani In Tucked 121
Barani In Piked 122
Half In One and Three-Quarter Front
    Somersault Tucked 123
Half In Half Out Fliffus 124
Half In Half Out Piked 126
Double Front Somersault Tucked with One
    and a Half Twists in the Second
    Somersault (Rudi Out Tucked) 127
Double Front Piked with One and a Half
    Twists Out (Rudi Out Piked) 128
Full In Back Out Fliffus 128
Back In Full Out Fliffus 130
Full In Full Out Fliffus 132
Full In Half Out Fliffus 133
Full In One and a Half Out Fliffus (Full In
    Rudi Out) 135
Half In One and a Half Twisting Front Out
    Fliffus 136
Double Ball Out with Half Twist Out (Ball
    Out Half Out) 137
Triple Front Somersault with Half Twist
    Out, Tucked (Triffus) 139

9 Physics Definitions; Principles of Motion; Illustrations of Principles 140

Physics Terms 143
Examples of Twisting in Mid-Air 145
Axes of Rotation 146
Rotation by Leaning 146
Rotation by Displacement 146
Eccentric Force About the Longitudinal
    Axis 146

Eccentric Force About the Lateral
  Axis 147
Eccentric Force About the Longitudinal and
  Lateral Axis 147
Transfer of Angular Momentum 148
Conservation of Momentum 148
Transfer of Angular Momentum 149
Relative Moment of Inertia Twisting
  Technique 149

10 Trampoline Safety 150

Causes of Accidents 150
Decision-Making Process in Learning and
  Teaching 150
Contributory Causes of Accidents 152

**11 Warm Up: General Principles for the
Coach or Teacher** 153

The Aim of 'Warm Up' 153
What Happens Physiologically 153
Psychological Effects of 'Warm up' 154

12 Sports Injury 155

Impact Injuries 155
Leverage or Strain Injuries 155
Overload Injuries 155
Factors Influencing Injury in Sport 155
Age of Participants 156

**13 Basic First Aid and Emergency
Procedures** 157

Minor Problems 157
More Serious Problems 158
Very Serious Injuries 158

**14 The Learning and Teaching of
Skill** 160

Personal Factors of the Pupil 160
Skill Learning and Other Factors Affecting
  the Acquisition of Skill 164
The Analysis of Skill 168
The Effects of Stress on the Learning
  Skill and the Performance of the
  Pupil 171
Signs of Stress in the Athlete
  or Competitor 174

15 The Tariff System 175

Tariffing Principles 175

16 The Development of Routines 177

Graded Routines 177
The Learning of Routines 178

17 Trampoline Terminology 185

Index 189

Foreword

Trampolining for Coaches and Performers is uniquely valuable because both author and illustrator have wide practical experience as top jumpers at the highest skill levels.

Rob Walker, by over twenty years of unbroken work in various roles as student, performer, teacher, coach, expert witness, organiser, promoter and non-resigning administrator, has achieved a great deal for the sport of trampolining.

In this comprehensive and authoritative manual – superbly illustrated by Jeff, his son – Rob covers all aspects of performance and coaching, from the vital elementary basics to the very latest and most advanced skills. It is full of sound, practical advice and of commonsense about safety, and its easy to follow logical analysis clears up many hitherto technical ambiguities.

Not everybody will agree with everything in this book, but that is why it is worth reading: differences of opinion make contests and competition possible. The conflict of competitive approaches and methods reveals, tests and helps perpetuate the most appropriate techniques.

With this important reference book, Rob and Jeff have probably given us the best single contribution to our sport so far. It brings us all quickly up-to-date, and is a must for both performers and coaches alike.

Ted Blake
Founder of the British Trampoline Federation

Acknowledgements

Illustrations by Jeff Walker.
Routines by Bert Scales.
Basic emergency procedures by Dr S McDonald MB, PhD, MRCS, FRCP, former Secretary to the Technical Committee of the BTF.
Cover photograph by Supersport Photographs.
Reading of text by Gerald Ramshaw and Judith Murrell

Introduction

The aim of this book is to provide an easily understandable source of information for trampolining coaches and pupils, and for others who may have an interest in the sport.

Although I have been a coach for many years, I have never been able to find a book on trampolining which would give me what I would call 'how to do it' information. The main section of this book covers a large number of skills, giving detailed illustration about how to learn to perform them. Several approaches to the learning of a skill are presented and, wherever possible, an appraisal of each approach is given. Obviously, some approaches will be more popular than others, but it is hoped that the material is set out in such a way that both coaches and performers will be able to move ahead successfully whichever they choose. It is intended that the principles used will provide readers with a logical and mechanically correct system for progressing smoothly from the lowest level of performance to reach their own highest potential.

It is also intended that the book will serve as a reference work for those who wish to take coaching awards. The information on teaching methods, safety precautions, support methods and mechanics should be sufficient for students at all levels of coaching schemes.

Trampolining for coaches and performers is the result of the experience I have gained in the twenty years of fun I have had in performing and coaching. I hope that my experience will be passed on and that it will, in some way, return a little to the sport from which I have derived so much pleasure. It is a fact that a teacher is influenced by those with whom he or she is in contact. I would, therefore, like to thank all those with whom I have practised, since they indirectly have contributed to this book. I hope it will repay their efforts on my behalf through the beneficial effect of its contents on future coaches and performers.

Rob Walker

1

Safety Code for all who Supervise, Teach or Take Part in Trampolining

The Hall and Equipment

The trampoline should be sited away from any overhead projections or walls, and any objects under the trampoline should be removed. For basic skills and supported somersaults for beginners the old type school gymnasium, about 16 feet high, is acceptable. For high and competition level work the height will need to be 20–25 ft (6–8m). Light from windows should not dazzle pupils or spotters. There should be space to store the trampolines away from the main hall. If not, the trampolines should be kept locked to avoid unsupervised or unauthorised use.

Normally two sizes of trampoline are in use in Britain, the 77a measuring 15 × 9ft (4.6 × 2.7m) and the Goliath measuring 17 × 10ft (5 × 3m). The 77a is 36in. (91cm) high and the Goliath 39in. (100cm). The trampoline used for international competition is slightly larger and slightly higher. It has safety decks at each end which can be clamped to the ends of the frame and are required by international rules as published by the International Trampoline Federation.

The main types of bed are the solid, the 1-inch (24mm), the ½-inch (12mm), the ¼-inch (6mm) and string or plastic mesh. Competition beds are marked to help the trampolinist with visual orientation. The centre is indicated by a cross and, more recently, by a rectangular box 2 × 1m lengthways on the bed. Steel springs or rubber cables are used

for the suspension systems. The frames should be padded with suitable pads supplied by the manufacturers. There are three types of pad: standard, for the frame only; wide, to cover the safety sides used for spotting; and cover all (now recommended by the BSI), to cover the springs.

Checking the Equipment

Before use, or at least weekly, the following should be checked.

[a] *Roller stands* for free swivelling and running castors and freely pivoting hooks. Castors should be firmly fixed in the roller stands.

[b] *Leg braces and chains* for security and proper adjustment.

[c] *Frame* for proper alignment, no bowing along the sides and the *hinges* free from cracks or excessive wear. No wear on the anchor bars from the hooks on the suspension.

[d] *Pads* for tears or splits, loose or missing frame clips, soft areas giving little protection to anyone landing in that section.

[e] *Springs or cables* hooks to be downwards and the tension to be even with all the rest of the suspension.

Beds

[a] Tears or thin areas in any of the fabric.

[b] Breaks in the webbing or loose stitching which could allow a toe or finger to penetrate.

[c] Uneven centre lines due to uneven tension. This can be cured for some time by moving the springs or cables around to even up the tension.

[d] Worn or broken nylon anchor bars around the bed.

[e] Excessive shrinkage of the bed causing very high tension.

All damage or wear should be reported to the proper authority and the manufacturer for repair. The trampoline should be taken out of use if it could prove a danger to any pupil or employee.

Folding and Unfolding the Trampoline

The folding and unfolding of trampolines should only be undertaken by authorised and trained persons. Trampolines are very heavy and the beds are under considerable tension. Care must be taken, therefore, to see that all unfolding and tensioning of the beds, release of bed tension and folding of frames is carried out in such a way that no person is in danger from swiftly moving or falling heavy metal parts.

When unfolding use at least two persons; one person should be in charge of the whole operation. Tilt the frame and lower one of the legs to the ground. Spread the tram-poline legs until the chains are taut and then remove the roller stands, keeping the chains taut so that the trampoline cannot collapse. Lift the upper end of the frame and lower slowly into the level position. Raise the other end and pull down to the level position, stretching the suspension in order to tension the bed. Alternatively both ends of the frame can be raised to vertical and lowered together. This method is easier when the suspension is very tight. Put all the leg braces into position and check them before anyone is allowed to use the trampoline.

To fold, again use at least two people. Release the leg braces. Both people are needed to break the tension by lifting one end section of the frame. The tension may be very high and care must be taken not to let the section rise quickly out of control. It is safer to raise both ends of the frame together, by using two or four people. The tension in the suspension will easily lift both end sections to about 45°. Continue until both are vertical. Although heavy, they can be balanced in the upright position. Fold to the horizontal, resting one on the other. Make sure that elbows are held clear of the frame and hands are positioned with the heel under the frame and fingers pointing outwards to avoid trapping them. Replace the roller stands in the frame. Move to the end last folded and raise the frame by the legs until the roller stands swing into place. This may be done by raising one side at a time or the whole frame at once, using more than one person. When the frame is supported by the roller stands swing the end you are holding down towards the floor so that the leg farthest away swings under the bed. Walk forward lifting the legs and frame: fold the lower leg up under the one you are holding so that it is held in place. Make sure the frame is upright and held by the hooks on the roller stands.

> NEVER PULL THE TRAMPOLINE TOWARDS YOU WHEN FOLDING IT UP. IT COULD BE TIPPED OVER AND FALL ON TOP OF YOU.
>
> PUT THE TRAMPOLINE AWAY OR LOCK THE FRAME.

The Teacher

All those teaching or supervising trampolining should have a trampolining coaching certificate or should have attended a coaching or safety course.

The teacher should never allow any:

[a] jumping on the trampoline without permission or without 4 spotters or crash mats as alternative protection;

[b] fooling around on the trampoline;

[c] eating or drinking on the trampoline;

[d] participation without sports clothing*;

[e] doubles work without permission;

[f] somersaulting without permission;

[g] new skills without checking the readiness of the pupil and without using progressions;

[h] use of the rig without checking the fitting, the ropes, swivels, buckles and the ability to hold the weight of the pupil;

[i] first attempts at multiple, or multiple twisting somersaults without the use of the rig and crash mats;

[j] jumping for long periods: 45 seconds to 1 minute is long enough;

[k] accident to go unreported.

The Performer

[a] Never unfold the trampoline without permission from the person authorised to be in charge.

[b] Do not practise alone.

[c] Pay attention at all times when spotting for others.

[d] Do not attempt moves beyond your ability.

[e] Do not get into competition with other performers.

[f] Listen to the advice of the person in charge of the group.

If all the above precautions are taken trampolining should be a safe and enjoyable activity for all involved. Most of them are common sense and are carried out automatically. An analysis of accidents which have happened will indicate that one, or more, of the advised procedures have been ignored.

---

*This will include shorts, track suits without hoods or leotards. For beginners track suits will protect the knees and elbows from abrasion on front drops and hands and knee drops. Small children should wear gymnastic or trampoline shoes or non-slip socks to prevent their toes from slipping through the holes in the webbed beds (especially the 6mm bed), trapping the foot and causing an accident. Nylon socks can slip and should be avoided. Adults, whose toes will not poke through the webbing so easily, may not need to wear any footwear other than to help keep the bed clean or in competition to conform with the International competition rules. Performers should also be told not to push their fingers through the webbing, since this could cause injury to the fingers.

2

Basic Jumping Skills

The first skill needed for trampolining is that of jumping. Start by swinging the arms backwards to give a little lift (Figure 1a) and then land in the position shown in Figure 1b. Push the legs down into the bed and swing the straight arms forward, and up, approximately to shoulder height (Figure 1c). In swingtime work the arms tend to be used at take-off from the position shown in Figure 1d up to the position shown by the dotted line. It is also popular to swing the arms up above the head (Figure 1e). Care must be taken not to over-extend the shoulders.

Use of the eyes is most important. Loss of visual contact can lead to panic through being LOST. Keep visual contact whenever possible. The guidelines in Figures 2 and 3 will help.

A flexed, balanced landing position helps towards a straight upward jump (Figure 4a). Make sure that the body is extended and the legs fully stretched as the body leaves the bed (Figure 4b). Hold the shoulders firm and do not attempt to lift them in order to jump higher. Keep the body segments in line and firm, with the seat firmly contracted and the head in line to avoid the ugly shape shown in Figure 4c.

Many beginners bounce with stiff legs (Figure 5a) rather than jump from the flexed

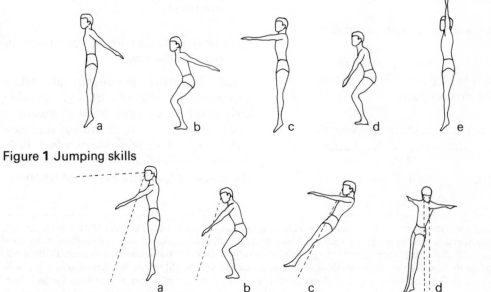

Figure 1 Jumping skills

Figure 2 Areas of visual contact

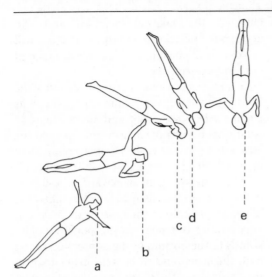

Figure 3 Visual contact whilst twisting

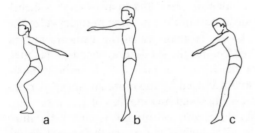

Figure 4 Balanced body position

the legs fly up, as fast as the shoulders drop, leading to over rotation (Figure 5d), which would be dangerous.

Arm Action at Take-off

One of the most controversial subjects discussed amongst coaches and performers seeking success is that of arm action before, during and after take-off. There is no doubt that arm action is very important to all performance but very few people can agree what is efficient, let alone most efficient.

There is a distinct difference between the action used in the performance of a single move and that used in swingtime or routines. In the performance of a single move the performer can concentrate easily on each aspect of the move. During the preliminary jumps, once a steady jumping height has been reached, all thought is on the actual take-off. The arm action, although it can make or break the move, is reasonably easy to carry out in the style the performer thinks best. Some will pull down on forward moves, having left the arms high on the last descent, and some will lift them a little, to try to get maximum height and direction, as the move is started. To the experienced coach it is easy to see the result of these slightly different actions in the different phasing or pattern of the subsequent skill. The action attempting to lift tends to be a little higher and the main part of the skill tends to be better phased. Figure

leg starting position. The stiff legs do not prevent an easy low level bouncing action which may seem suitable for beginners. However, stiff legs limit the hip mobility of the body and the easy initiation of rotation. Figure 5b shows stiff-legged, straight bouncing, locked hips and rotation initiated by backward lean. As contact is lost (Figure 5c),

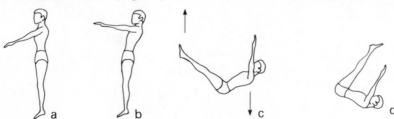

Figure 5 Stiff legged bouncing and lean

6a–g illustrates the most frequently observed sequence of arm use in forward take-offs in routine.

As the performer descends towards the bed, the arms lift to shoulder height or just above in relation to the trunk and the legs are bent, just before landing. Just before or just after landing, the arms are raised to a position in line with the trunk. The arms remain in this position whilst the performer sinks into the bed, and begin to be pulled down as the performer rebounds out of the bed.

It has been observed that the performer who delays the pull down, even a little, tends to gain more height during the take-off since the trunk is a little more vertical during the point of take-off and thus is aimed upwards instead of downwards. It is a problem for the coach who has to decide which technique is to be used. It is very tempting for both coach and performer to work on the early pull down on forward somersault take-offs. It may, however, be wiser to school the pupil to attempt to make some initial upward arm lift, however short in duration. Pulling down will give greater flexion at the waist and will not only cut height but will lead to travel if the arms reach too far forward. It will give plenty of rotational force but less height. There will be less acceleration potential since the body will be well bent at take-off, giving less difference

between the take-off position and the accelerated position. Consequently there will be less clear phasing and less appearance of ease in performance.

Alternatively the attempt to lift aims the body upwards, gives a more open shape as the body leaves the bed and alters the main rotational input power from the arms to the legs and bed via even less displacement than results from the arm pull down technique.

The arm swing in backward take-offs is different from that used in forward take-offs. The arm position in the descent to the bed is very similar but then, as the performer descends to the bottom of the depression of the bed, the arms tend to be held lower than in forward take-offs. By the time the bottom of the depression is reached the arms are high and already travelling in a backwards direction as part of the initiation of rotation for the take-off. In many cases the arms are moved well behind the shoulders, bent at the elbow, or the back is arched. All these body positions are used by the more advanced performers observed on cine film of European and World Championships. It is most difficult to decide which is the most efficient action for performance. It might help to realise that pupils differ in shape, amounts of strength in the different parts of their bodies, leverages and even ideas of what they are actually or

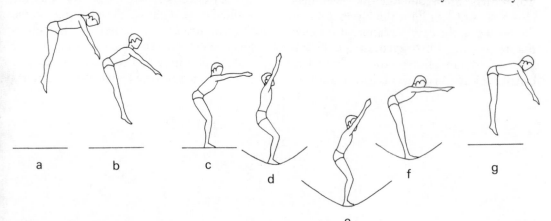

Figure **6** Arm action during the take-off for forward skills

supposedly performing. All these factors contribute to the type of arm action used by each performer.

Figures 7a–g illustrate the most frequently observed sequences of arm use during the take-off for backward skills in routine. In double somersaults there is usually a much more pronounced arching of the back by the time the performer has reached the point in the take-off sequence as shown in Figure 7f. This indicates the feeling that there is a need to gain much greater rotational force at take-off.

It is often the desire to gain greater rotational force at take-off which leads the performer to pull down early or to lean back excessively. The problem is to teach the performer a technique which gives maximum height with enough rotation for the move to be performed. There is a tendency in all the early stages of learning trampolining to attempt to create powerful rotation by pulling down into moves or by leaning. In many cases this is not checked at all by the coach and the performer is allowed to develop bad performance habits. This means that one part of the technique is over-emphasised at the expense of the other constituent parts. This in turn leads to a cumulative total error, which may be much more difficult to correct than the original isolated fault, since each

subsequent section of the skill has to be adjusted sequentially to avoid the effects of the original fault.

Since trampolining is still in a relatively early stage of development, although great strides have been made in levels of difficulty and performance, it is still necessary to keep observing and recording what the performers actually do whilst in contact with the bed and in the air. This must be set against what the coaches are trying to get them to do in training sessions in order that well-defined techniques may be developed. In this way beginners will be able to work on the recognised techniques and hopefully there will be a general raising of the level of performance. This in turn should lead to greater advances by the very talented, accompanied by further observation and recording to try to improve the work at beginner stage. This does not mean that people will not still experiment at all levels. It is important that a body of knowledge be recorded so comparison can be made via reference to the work done so far. It is then easily available for all in written form to save each coach having to start from scratch.

Figure 7 Arm action in a backward take-off

Rotation about the Lateral Axis (Initiated by Leaning)

Leaning is the way locomotion is initiated. Thus it might unconsciously be the way rotation and twist are automatically initiated. Look at the back drop initiation process to see what happens when you lean and why (Figures 5b–d). Displacement of hips gives rotational power through the eccentric thrust by the bed via the legs. Rotation should not be initiated by dropping the head.

Initiation of rotation by leaning

For front and back somersaults, swing arms up to approximately shoulder height (Figure 8a). Displace the hips forward or backwards only far enough to provide eccentric position of hips, without dropping the shoulders, at the time the return thrust of the bed takes place (Figures 8b and c).

This will give rotation without travel. Height will depend on the power of the leg push. Rotation also will depend upon this and upon the amount of eccentricity. More eccentricity will give more rotation, gained at the expense of height. This skill is important for optimum performance, combined with stability.

Rotation about the Longitudinal Axis (Twisting)

Twisting is easy if started correctly. Use the power of the trunk muscles to initiate your twist. Start to twist as the legs start to straighten whilst still in contact with the bed. Do not lean in your effort to set up a strong twist.

Start the twist with the arms out to the side. This enables the twist to be speeded up by pulling the arms into the body, using the already initiated twisting power, and avoids

Figure **8** Rotation about the lateral axis

Figure **9** Twisting about the longitudinal axis

the need to throw the arms hard across the body in the direction of the twist, which often leads to cast and loss of balance. Figure 9a shows the arms at greatest extent, giving most potential for increase of speed when arms are pulled in close.

Figure 9b shows the starting position of the body as twist is about to be initiated. There is flexion at the waist, knees, and ankles. Let the twist come easily, starting from the waist and going up the body as it straightens for the jump. Keep it smooth and easy.

Plain Jump

Possibly the plain jump is the most necessary in the performer's skill range. It is difficult to get easy height and requires constant practice. Note the use of the arms. They do help the depression of the bed (action–reaction).

In Figure 10a the performer is at the bottom of the depression, arms ready to help depress the bed a little more. Figure 10b, leaving the bed, shows the arms not yet at full extent of swing, the legs are straight, and the whole body is tight. Figure 10c illustrates the mid-point of the flight. It is sufficient to raise the arms no more than is shown here. If they are raised to the position in Figure 10f,

arching could possibly occur. Figure 10d shows the start of the descent to the bed, with the body taut and the arms in position for the next arm swing. Figure 10e illustrates the body on the bed, with legs bent already, depressing the bed, and about to depress it more by means of the leg push and arm swing. Aim for smooth, easy, controlled flight: do not try too hard for your height. Stopping is achieved by quickly bending the legs at the knees as in Figure 10e in order to kill the recoil of the bed.

Tucked Jump

This is the first of the basic skills after jumping. From a regular take-off (Figure 11a) stretch the body in flight, extending the arms above the head (Figure 11b). At the top of the jump grasp the shins with the hands and pull the legs into the chest momentarily. Release the legs and prepare for the next take-off.

Note in Figure 11 the balanced position of the body. There is also the obvious phasing of the move, with the tucked position adopted only at the top of the jump.

There is a tendency to initiate a little rotation if the performer attempts to pull the

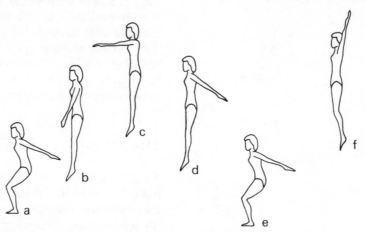

Figure **10** The plain jump

knees in to the chest too early. Get the feeling of straight flight upwards, then pull the knees in (Figures 11b and 11c). Return to the preparation for landing position (Figure 11d). Landing position is shown in Figure 11c.

The tucked position, as shown in Figure 11c, is not only preparation for the tucked somersault but a required position described in the International Rules.

Figure 11 The tucked jump

Piked Jump

The piked jump is another of the basic jumps. Once again it is practice for the piked

Figure 12 The piked jump

position in somersaults. It is also a required position described in the International Rules. The only difference from the tucked jump is the body position.

The body has to be folded at the waist to an angle of 90° or less. Legs are locked at the knees. Hands hold the legs as in Figure 12. They may however rest on the legs. Beginners' attempts to hold too near the toes tend to cause the performer to turn the toes up.

Make sure that the full extension is reached before attempting the piked position. An attempt too early may cause loss of balance. The hand position, as shown in Figure 12c, is helpful in maintaining a straight leg position: holding just behind the knees tends to cause some bending of the legs.

Piked Straddle Jump

This is useful as a fill in move or simple skill. It is not a practice for a somersault position. Start as a tucked or piked jump. Fold the body at the top of the jump. It is easier to reach the toes than on the piked jump since the legs will be apart in the piked position as in Figure 13c.

The three basic jumps (tucked, piked and straddle) are all shaped at the top of the jump in a swift decisive movement and there is an immediate return to the straight position just after the top of the flight is passed. They all give the first opportunities to practise phased skills. The flight, shape, downward flight can all be easily practised before moving on to phasing in more difficult skills.

Straight Jump with Half Twist

Twisting is a skill that is usually learned with difficulty. Rotation about the longitudinal axis requires less effort than is usually thought necessary. For the type of twist that is most frequently seen (twist initiated before

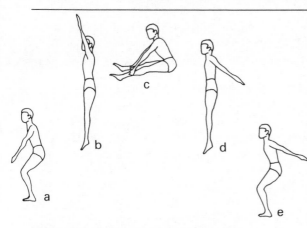

Figure **13** The piked straddle jump

momentum) (Figure 14d) until the landing is made in the opposite direction (Figure 14c). The twist must be smooth and fairly gentle. If this part of the skill is learned well the full twist will develop very easily from it.

Straight Jump with Full Twist

The jump with full twist is an easy progression from the half twist jump, the most important part of the skill being the initiation of the twist. This basic move gives another opportunity to practise phasing. It is essential to wait until the take-off has registered in the mind and to ensure that the twist is under way for at least a quarter to one-third of a turn (Figure 15a–c). At this point (Figure 15d) the arms are smoothly pulled in close to the chest so that they arrive there (Figures 15e and f) at the same time, with neither arm getting more effort applied to it. This could be classified as a delicate skill. The main fault seems to be wild use of the arms in an unco-ordinated fashion, in order to make the full twist.

The method is to bring the arms in, thus reducing the moment of inertia about the longitudinal axis and resulting in an increase in the speed of rotation. The wide spread of the arms in the initial starting position gives

the feet leave the bed) certain principles apply.

It is usually necessary to establish the direction of twist. Figure 14b shows a twist to the left. From the position shown in Figure 14f with arms stretched out sideways, the upper body is turned to the left as the jump is started (Figure 14g). This upper body movement initiates the twist to the left whilst still in contact with the bed. The arms must be kept straight and at shoulder level, and move as a unit with the upper body. The twist is started with the body as shown in Figure 14a. The body straightens, the twist is increased (Figures 15b and c); and as the body leaves, the twist carries on (transfer of

Figure **14** Straight jump with half twist

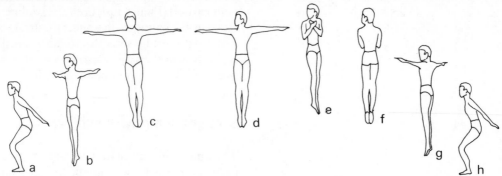

Figure **15** Straight jump with full twist

the potential for considerable increase in speed of rotation. Figures 15a–h show the sequence of arms and body action. The wide position of the arms in Figure 15g gives maximum deceleration before landing (Figure 15h). It is important to try to keep a smooth, easy flight during the whole movement. The arms can of course be moved in close to the body in any position the performer desires. For the trampoline the position in Figure 15e would seem to be mechanically economical and aesthetically pleasing.

Seat Drop

The seat drop is normally the first skill without a foot landing learned by a beginner. It is a very pleasant move to do and the first of the skills which can be done due to the nature of the apparatus.

From the standard starting position shown in Figure 16a the arms are swung up above the head and the feet taken backwards along the bed, keeping the legs straight (Figure 16b). As the body descends, the fold at the hips is increased until the legs are horizontal to the bed for the landing (Figure 16d). Note in Figure 16d that the trunk leans slightly backwards. To rebound to feet, push down and back on the hands (fingers always pointing forwards) and move the shoulders slightly forwards. This will give enough forward rotation (Figure 16e) to bring the body up to a standing position with the feet in the same position on the bed (Figure 16f).

Figure **16** Seat drop

Figure **17** Seat drop half twist to feet

Seat Drop Half Twist to Feet

Begin as for a normal seat drop (Figures 17a–d). From the seat landing position push down and back with the arms and hands and, as the body begins to rise (Figure 17e), throw the arms vigorously up and around in the direction in which you wish to twist. The vigour of the arms being swung in an upward direction helps straighten the body to make the twist easier. Figures 17f, g, h show the completion of the half twist and the landing.

In both the seat drop to feet and the seat drop half twist to feet, it is important to make sure that you begin to straighten the body as it begins to rise from the bed. This gives a smooth easy style of performance without jerking the body. Bringing the toes back along the red longitudinal centre line also helps to keep the whole movement square to the bed of the trampoline. The seat drop half twist to feet is the first skill involving twisting from a piked position as well as by purchase from the bed of the trampoline.

Half Twist to Seat Drop

The half twist to seat drop is a simple movement. From a standard balanced starting position (Figure 18a), swing the arms forward and upward, simultaneously turning the shoulders gently in the direction of the twist and taking the legs very gently backwards along the centre line of the bed (Figure 18b).

Figure **18** Half twist to seat drop

As the body rises into the air the gentle twist will carry on (Figure 18c) and the slight backward movement of the legs will cause a slight rotation about the lateral axis. This will enable the seat drop landing position to be made with a very slight backward tilt of the upper body (Figures 18d, e). From the landing position shown in Figure 18e it is simple to push backwards and down on the hands setting up a slight forward rotation to the feet (eccentric force). This movement should be done smoothly with a slow turn of the body giving an impression of ease.

Swivel Hips

The swivel hips is a very pleasing movement to perform and gives the first experience of twisting from a position other than the feet.

A regular seat drop is performed as in Figures 19a–d. From the seat drop landing position, the hands push back and down to set up slight forward rotation (eccentric force), the arms are swung up and forwards vigorously and the shoulders are twisted strongly in the direction of the desired twist (Figure 19e). It should be emphasised that the movement is a vigorous one. As the body straightens out in mid-flight the twist, initiated by the turning of the shoulders, partly against the resistance of the bed and partly

by the resistance of the legs. Twisting continues until the body is piked for the landing (Figures 19f–h). Trampolinists have recently given the name RMI (Relative Moment of Inertia) twisting to the type of twist initiated against the resistance of the legs. The legs are at right angles or less to the body and have a greater resistance to a turning force than the shoulders. Consequently the shoulders turn in the direction of twist, whilst the legs turn relatively less since they have greater mass and radius. As the body straightens, the resistance of the legs is reduced and the whole body turns. Piking arrests the twist.

Seat Drop, Full Twist to Seat Drop

This move can be accomplished in two ways using two different twisting techniques. Figure 20 shows RMI (Relative Moment of Inertia) twisting technique. Figure 21 shows twisting by means of eccentric force produced by pushing on one hand against the bed. Figure 20a shows what is probably the best simple example of RMI twisting.

Practise a seat drop as shown in Figure 16f. Make sure that there is a slight lean back. Do not drop from too great a height since it is easy to jar the back. Allow the body to rebound into the air and land again in the seat drop position. The body will automatically

Figure **19** The swivel hips

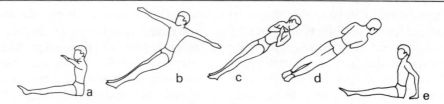

Figure **20** Seat drop full twist to seat drop: first method

straighten out a little to maintain equilibrium. When this preliminary skill has been mastered, drop on to the seat and on contact turn the head and shoulders in the desired direction of twist. Make sure that there is no sideways lean as the shoulders and outstretched arms are twisted. As the body rises from the bed and straightens, the arms are pulled in close to the body, making an easy acceleration of the twist. Once again it is important not to let the body deviate too far from the positions shown in Figures 20b, d, e. The arms are placed behind the seat for the landing (Figure 20e).

The twisting power is produced by the upper body being twisted against the larger radius of the legs, whose resistance is increased by contact with the bed. As the body leaves the bed and straightens and the arms are pulled in, the radius about the longitudinal axis shortens and the twist is easily completed.

The second method is by pushing against the bed outside the centre of the body, with one hand, to produce the required eccentric twisting force. From the position shown in Figure 21a, practise raising the body to a straight position with a low bounce (Figure 21b), then return to the seat drop. Once the above has been mastered push hard on the right hand (Figure 21c). Keep pushing

until the body turns and the hand can no longer push against the bed, at the same time straightening the body. The right hand will finish behind the body and the left hand in front (Figure 21d). Make sure that there is no lean in the direction of twist or any attempt to throw the right arm across the body. This will slow up the twist and cause an action–reaction adjustment of the body. As the twist is completed return to the position shown in Figure 21a for the landing. The whole move may also be carried out by using the left hand, causing the body to turn to the right. Any lean results in an off centre line landing.

Front Drop (Straight)

The front drop is the most important move the beginner learns connected with forward rotation. A front drop is one-quarter of a front somersault. The principle of the application of eccentric force is now used to initiate forward rotation. Figure 22a shows the basic balanced stance ready for take-off. The arms are swung forward and up to just about shoulder height. They do not swing forwards only. The hips are moved backwards as take-off commences and the feet are taken backwards along the centre line

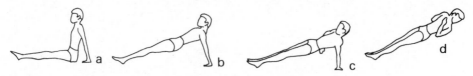

Figure **21** Seat drop full twist to seat drop: second method

of the trampoline. The body should rise up into the air as a unit. It should not be noticeable that the shoulders are dropping downwards. As the body leaves the bed it should straighten out and rotate fairly slowly as shown in Figures 22b and c. Remember, once rotation has been initiated rotation will occur continuously in the air until the body lands on the bed, or until some other outside force is applied to it.

The landing should be as shown in Figure 22d, forearms and palms flat, elbows not pushed into the bed, body flat from chest to knees. Legs are bent at the knee before landing is made to enable leg kick downwards to initiate rotation backwards to the feet (Figures 22e and f). Once more eccentric force is applied by the kick down of the lower leg and transferred by the locking of the hips to the whole of the body (transfer of momentum).

It is acceptable in the early stages for the learner to rotate through the quarter somersault in a slightly bent body position to allow for adjustment of the rotation speed (variable moment of inertia, shorter for increase of rotational speed, longer for decrease of rotational speed) (Figure 23). At first there may be too much or too little rotation. Excess rotation will cause a landing on the upper chest or face and painful arching of the back. Too little will cause the legs to land first and the chest and face to be thrown powerfully into the bed causing considerable discomfort. As skill increases, the body should be straightened immediately after take-off.

Some people may experience difficulty in learning a comfortable front drop landing. It is useful to start from the hands and knees in an all-fours position. This gives a lower starting position and less likelihood of a heavy landing, especially if the landing is at the wrong angle. Start as shown in Figure 24a with the hands slightly ahead of the shoulders and the knees behind the hips. Without leaning forward at the shoulders push down on the feet and raise the hips (Figure 24b). As the hips reach the top of their rise move the legs backwards, still

Figure **22** Front drop (straight)

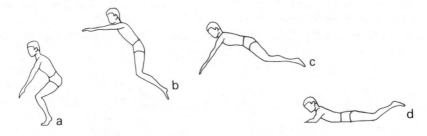

Figure **23** Front drop, bent body (early stages)

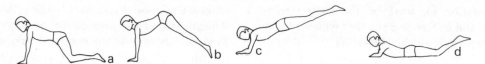

Figure **24** Front drop landing

keeping the shoulders well behind the hands (Figure 24c). Allow the body to drop vertically down to landing (Figure 24d).

With all versions of the front drop it is essential to get the feeling that the legs are moving backwards whilst getting the shoulders to move upwards. Travel will then be eliminated and the front drop should be easy to control. Having started from the kneeling position it is sometimes useful to try and drop into the hands and knees position and then rebound to the front drop landing position. A nervous person may feel happier approaching the front drop in these stages.

An alternative method of starting the pupil on a front drop is to adopt the stance shown in Figure 25. Figure 25a shows the pupil in a body position which is the same as it would be just after take-off. Note that the body is straight, the arms are in the landing position and one bent leg supports the body. The technique is to push down into the bed with the supporting leg and as the body rises to lift that leg up to the same level as the straight leg. It is important not to let the shoulders and the head drop towards the bed from the position shown in Figure 25c, or a dive take-off will occur. Figure 25d shows the landing position once more. The legs are ready for the down-

ward kick in order to bring the body rotating up straight to feet. Tightening of the gluteal muscles helps to ensure that the body is kept straight throughout the movement.

The above method has been used successfully with some nervous pupils. It is necessary to try to keep the pupil calm as the movement is started to help avoid any rushed and possibly diving take-off.

Front Drop Tucked

Many people first learned the front drop using the tucked position in mid-flight as an easy way to get a horizontal position in the air in preparation for landing. It is easier, however, to learn the front drop tucked after learning the front drop straight.

From a standard take-off (see Figure 26), pull the body into a tucked position, with the hands grasping the shins. As soon as the top of the lift is reached release the hands and straighten the body so that, as the descent is made, any slight rotation is practically stopped by the straightening of the body. It is important to try to let the body lift into the air for the take-off rather than to drop the upper body for tuck position. This move could be used as a practice for tucking in

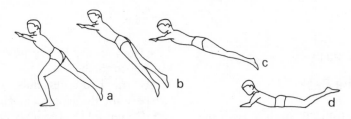

Figure **25** Front drop from one leg

preparation for work on the front somersault, and in any case is a skill which adds to the repertoire of the performer.

Figure 26 Front drop tucked

Front Drop Piked

This variation (see Figure 27) of the front drop is easily performed by a beginner who drops the top of the body in reaching for the ankles to achieve the piked position. However, if a well-lifted move is desired it becomes a little more difficult to perform this move. The body must be directed upwards with the arms well lifted and the body straight until well into the flight. Then the body is folded at the hips and the hands reach down to grasp the legs at or near the ankles.

Figure 27 Front drop piked

Bouncing on the Back

This is a very useful skill, since it gives the basic techniques for all those moves which involve a take-off from a back landing. A very delicate use of the application of eccentric force to rebound on the spot and to initiate rotation, and sometimes twist, is needed.

Figure 28a gives an indication of the starting movement. From the back landing position the legs and the seat are pushed upwards until the seat and lower back are clear. This

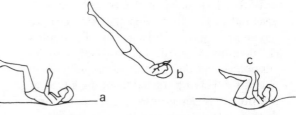

Figure 28 Bouncing on the back

will give a considerable depression to the bed, which in turn will give a good lift to the body. The arms can be held in the position shown or even wider if twisting movements are to be initiated.

After take-off the body is straightened and the legs pushed strongly upwards (Figure 28b), the eyes looking along the body. To get to this straight position the buttocks must be squeezed firmly together. It is important to work on extending the body to this position, since it will mean that there is already the intention to extend well when the movement

is started on the bed, producing a stronger push into the bed.

As the body descends it is folded to prepare for the landing and the next push-off. Do not fold as the body reaches the bed, but before. The body must reach the bed folded and well tensed (Figure 28c). The bed can then be depressed by the full weight of the body as it lands and further depressed by the upward extension of the legs; thus a good height can be easily attained and maintained. Make sure that the arms are not held too high on landing or they will tend to be left behind as the body leaves the bed. This will not help any twisting or rotational movement desired after take-off.

Flat Back Drop from Feet

Many pupils have difficulty in accepting that a back drop is performed by moving the feet forwards instead of dropping the shoulders backwards. The flat back drop from feet will often help to change this idea and to consolidate the skill of moving the feet foward as a result of forward hip displacement.

Figure 29a shows the normal starting

Figure **29** Flat back drop from feet

stance. It may be set a little lower for some pupils. In Figure 29b the pupil has jumped into the air a little way and is pushing the lower legs forwards. Figures 29c and d show the body dropping completely straight to land in the flat back drop position. To hold the body straight the buttocks must be tightly contracted and the stomach muscles held tight so that there is no arching. It is difficult to return to the feet from this landing without letting the body fold. The very nervous pupil could perform this move on the crash mat for the first few attempts. The power of the 'kip' can be increased or decreased as the coach measures the need.

Back Drop (Straight)

The back drop is the next movement involving backward rotation. It is most important to learn this movement correctly. Backward rotation is initiated by using the principle of the application of eccentric force. From the standard balanced stance shown in Figure 30a the arms are swung forward and up, the legs are straightened and the hips are moved forward to coincide with the leg push. The take-off is made with the body in the position shown in Figure 30b. The shoulders and head are over the feet and the hips are forward of the longitudinal axis.

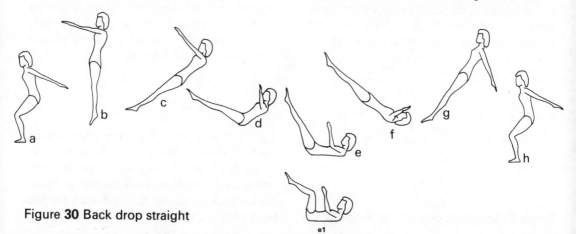

Figure **30** Back drop straight

There is sufficient displacement of the hips to cause the return thrust of the bed, via the straightened legs, to initiate enough rotation backwards to give 90° rotation (Figures 30c and d), landing on the back as in Figure 30e. From the position shown in Figure 30e, the straight legs can be pushed up and forwards and the body extended as in Figure 30f, so that a forward rotational force is set up by the eccentric action of the legs. The momentum in the legs is transferred to the whole body when the legs are stopped by muscular action (contraction of stomach and gluteal muscles). The body rises as a rigid unit and rotates as shown in Figure 30g. The landing on the feet should be in the same place as that from which the take-off was made (Figure 30h).

Figure 30e1 shows the landing position used if more height is needed. The legs are extended sharply from the knee in an upwards direction and then they are pushed away in one continuous movement to take up the position shown in Figure 30f.

Figures 31a–c show a take-off, modified to help the beginner. From a low position (Figure 31a) the knees are jumped horizontally forwards, the arms are swung forward and up, and the body is held firm in the position shown in Figure 31b. As the body rises into the air the rotation initiated by the horizontal movement of the knees will continue until the body reaches the bed (a body in motion will carry on in the same motion until acted upon by another force). After take-off no further adjustment is needed until the

landing is about to be made. Throwing the legs into the air should be avoided since this gives too much rotation. Over rotation could cause an unpleasant, or even dangerous, landing high up on the shoulders.

It is sometimes necessary for the coach to use some measure of support for pupils who throw back extensively (see support methods). Notice in all the figures the head is held forward and the bed is kept in view all the time.

Back Drop Tucked

The pupil who has successfully learned the back drop straight should have little difficulty in mastering the back drop tucked. Care should be taken that the take-off is gentle and nearly vertical (Figure 32b) so

Figure **32** Back drop tucked

that the pronounced tucking of the body (Figure 32c) does not cause over rotation. As soon as the tucked position has been fully attained the body is straightened and adjustment made for the landing.

Back Drop Piked

The back drop piked is similar in take-off to the back drop tucked; that is, the pupil must remember that the sharp piking of the body will cause an acceleration of rotation in flight, thus a slightly slower take-off than for the back drop straight must be made. The piking

Figure **31** Modified take-off for the beginner

Figure **33** Back drop piked

should take place at the top of the flight rather than an early lift up of the legs at take-off (Figures 33c and d). When performed with good phasing, this move is very attractive and, like the back drop tucked, can be used as a preparation move for later skills.

Back Drop from One Leg

Another progression for the back drop is the back drop performed with a one leg take-off. As with the front drop from one leg, this variation is designed to help the beginner who is not getting much success with the back drop from two feet by letting the head and shoulders drop backwards.

Take the stance shown in Figure 34a. The body is held in a balanced position, the standing leg bent, ready to push down into the bed. As this leg is pushed down, the upper leg is held still and the shoulders are not dropped back. The bed will return the push down in the form of lift and the standing leg is raised only to the height of the upper leg and bent to match its shape and

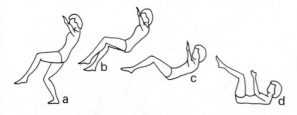

Figure **34** Back drop from one leg

position (Figure 34b). Figure 34c shows the whole body descending into the bed ready to land in the position shown in Figure 34d. The pupil must give sufficent lift of the lower leg to make sure that a landing is not made on the base of the spine so that the head jerks back, but must be careful not to move this leg as if performing an overhead kick in soccer. This could lead to over rotation and a landing on the neck or head. From Figure 34d the pupil can either bounce on the back or rebound to feet; the landing position is suitable for either choice.

Half Twist to Front Drop

From a regular starting balanced position turn the head in the direction of twist and look at the central area of the bed, which runs the length of it. Take off turning the shoulders, in addition to the head, as the take-off is started (Figures 35a–c). Make sure that the arms are held out sideways to give good form and the possibility of acceleration in flight. Let the body carry on rotating slowly, keeping the eyes on the central area until you are ready to land. Bring the arms into the regular landing position for the front drop. Make sure that the twist is only gentle, since the pulling in of the arms for the landing may cause a slight overtwisting. Figure 35c shows the arms in flight, Figure 35d pulling in for the landing and Figure 35e the final landing position.

Looking at the central area of the bed as a

Figure **35** Half twist to front drop

reference point throughout the movement helps orientation, which is most important in twisting moves.

For a very nervous person a much lower start can be made than that shown in Figure 35a. The body may also be twisted round much more whilst the feet are still in contact with the bed.

Half Twist to Back Drop

This move usually proves much more difficult to control than the half twist to front drop. Once again the eyes are focused on the central area of the bed. They stay focused on it until just before the moment of landing. This means that the head is still facing the bed during most of the flight. This is a similar technique to that used for the barani.

From a regular take-off position (Figure 36a) start turning the body with the arms held wide whilst the feet are still in contact, leading to Figure 36b. The body continues in

flight still watching the line on the bed (Figure 36c). Only as the body is ready to land (Figure 36d) is the head turned to the front with the vision directed downwards, looking through the body at the bed. Turning away from the bed too soon tends to cause a feeling of insecurity and loss of form. Keep the body straight in flight to avoid the legs swinging sideways, causing a rebound to the side on landing. Bend the legs on landing and kick upwards and forwards to get a good high rebound to feet.

Front Drop, Half Twist to Feet

The front drop half twist to feet is a very tricky movement to learn. A regular front drop is performed (Figures 37a and b), making sure that the legs are bent ready for the downward kick which will bring the body up to the feet. Practise coming up to the feet with the body straight by ensuring that abdominals and back muscles are kept tight.

Figure **36** Half twist to back drop

Figure **37** Front drop half twist to feet

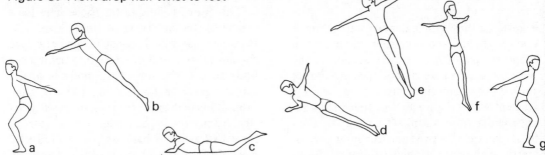

The twist is produced by pushing the left hand (Figure 37c) down into the bed. This will cause the body to turn to the left as it rises (Figure 37d). Immediately after leaving the bed keep the arms held out sideways so that they can be pulled in to produce a full twist. Figures 37e and f depict the body showing the arms held out in flight, and Figure 37g shows them ready for the next take-off.

It is quite difficult to combine the two techniques of keeping the body tense for a straight flight up to the feet and pushing on the bed with one hand only to produce the twist. It is an important skill since it is one of the progressions for learning twisting somersaults from the stomach.

Back Drop, Half Twist to Feet

This move is easier than the front drop half twist to feet. It is also a progression for a number of other moves, e.g. 'baby fliffus and corkscrew'. A regular back drop is performed (Figures 38a–c). From the landing position shown in Figure 38d, the legs are beaten up and away, and, at the same time, the shoulders are twisted in the direction of twist (Figure 38e). As the body rises, twisting, the arms are again held out to the side, to enable the twist to be accelerated (Figures 38f, g). Figure 38h shows the landing position with arms ready for the next move. It is important to have good positioning of the arms on the back landing position (Figure 38d). This helps to keep the arms under control on landing and gives a suitable starting position.

Remember to turn the shoulders immediately on contact with the bed. If this is not done it will be difficult to obtain a smooth twist or good body position in flight, thus spoiling the appearance of the body in flight. Good twisting depends upon a straight body after the twist has been set up. Any bending or arching of the body slows up the twist.

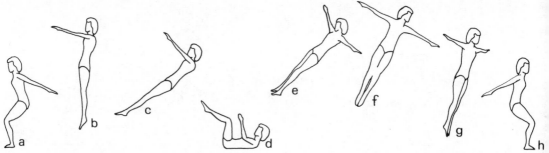

Figure **38** Back drop half twist to feet

Full Twist to Back Drop

Figure 39a shows the balanced starting position. As the take-off is started, the head and shoulders are turned in the direction of the twist and the eyes are kept on the bed (Figure 39b). As the body rises into the air the arms are kept wide (Figure 39c) so that the twisting angular momentum set up may be used to accelerate the twist as the moments of inertia of the outstretched arms are reduced (Figure 39d, e) by bringing the arms in close to the body. Note that the arms are not brought in until the body is at least half-way through the flight. In Figure 39e, the body has reached the horizontal and the last part of the twist is about to be completed (Figure 39f), and the arms are spread wide to slow down the speed of twist. Figure 39g shows the body in the just landed position. The legs are bent and the feet medium height ready to

kick up and away for a return to the feet.

This move is simple for those who have mastered the half twist to front drop. The beginner may find it easier to turn and face the central area of the bed slightly behind the body so that the top of the body is in the starting position for the half twist to back drop. This makes the movement visually easier. Alternatively the performer can start as for a half twist to back drop and gradually work further round to a starting position facing in the opposite direction, thus making a full twist. Both progressions are useful, one suiting some pupils and one suiting others.

Full Twist to Front Drop

This is a tricky move because of the problem of visual orientation. Practise the half twist to back drop making sure that the eyes are kept

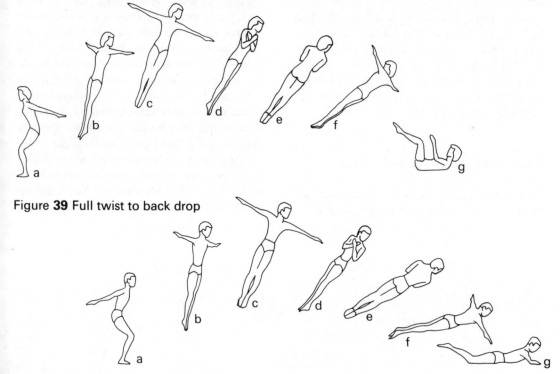

Figure **39** Full twist to back drop

Figure **40** Full twist to front drop

focused on the bed until just before the landing as in Figures 40a–c. This is the key to the full twist. Practise overturning the twist a little to get used to the idea of going further round. Take this practice time to turn the head at the last moment in the direction of twist. Keep the arms well apart so that when pulled in (Figures 40d and e) the last part of the twist is easily and quickly completed. Open out the arms and re-focus on the bed (Figure 40f) for the landing shown in Figure 40g. Make sure the bed is sighted for stages a–e, the head is turned only at the stage shown in Figure 40f. Under or over rotation about the lateral axis will cause very unpleasant landings. Use of the crash mat is advisable.

Front Drop, Full Twist to Feet

From a good front drop landing (Figure 41a), kick down sharply towards the bed with the lower legs, at the same time contracting the buttocks, so that the body starts to rise. Push down hard on the left arm so that the body starts to turn in the direction shown in Figure 41b. As the body leaves the bed, extend the arms sideways (Figure 41c) so that the rate of twist may be accelerated when the arms are pulled in close to the body (Figures 41d, e). Extend the arms sideways as approximately three-quarters of the twist is

completed (Figure 41f). This action will decrease the speed of twist for an easy landing (Figure 41g), with the performer ready for the next take-off.

It is important to remember that, in order to twist in the direction shown in the figures (to the left), it is necessary to push powerfully down into the bed with the left arm. The push causes the left shoulder to come out of the bed first. The body must be kept straight by contraction of the thighs, buttocks and abdominals so that the twist is not retarded. This move is fairly difficult to perform with ease and a certain amount of thoughtful practice is necessary for success. It is useful as a build-up when learning the full twisting cody.

Back Drop, Full Twist to Feet

From a good back drop (Figure 42a) practise a straight rebound to feet. Try to avoid any arching or piking. This requires a powerful up kick. As the kick is made, the head and shoulders are turned in the direction shown, keeping the arms outstretched as shown in Figures 42b, c. Figures 42d–f show the acceleration and deceleration of the rate of twist and Figure 42g shows the landing position. For success it is important that the twist is initiated whilst in contact with the bed from the

Figure 41 Front drop full twist to feet

Figure **42** Back drop full twist to feet

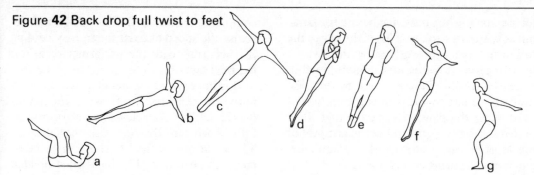

shoulders to the hips. If the twist is started too late, it is apparent from the trailing right arm and shoulder and difficulty in completing the full twist (action–reaction between the upper and lower half of the body).

Front Drop to Back Drop

Mastery of the front drop to feet is the key to the above move. A good downward leg kick is necessary from the position shown in Figure 43a. Make sure that the legs are stretched and taut and the buttocks are contracted to keep the body straight and tight (Figure 43b), so that no rotational power is lost. Tucking (Figure 43c) speeds up the rotation. As the body reaches the position shown in Figure 43d the body is extended a little to slow up the rotation, enabling a landing to be made as in Figure 43e. The landing position is the ready for take-off position for any move with forward rotation or backward rotation from the back.

Notice that the head is not thrown back nor is there any folding of the body at the hips until a good straight take-off has been made. This helps to ensure that enough rotational momentum has been gained before tucking to accelerate speed or rotation.

The above is an important stage in the learning of the cody. As more proficiency is gained the pupil should try to pass through the positions shown in Figures 43c and d with the body straight. This will help to ensure that sufficient power is available for the complete somersault backwards from stomach to feet.

Back Drop to Front Drop

Figure 44a shows the landing position on the back which will enable the pupil to rebound up to feet on the same spot on the bed from which the take-off and the back landing were made. The back drop has to be performed without any backward travel to ensure that

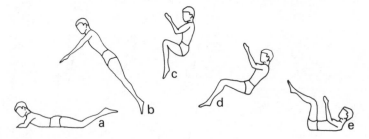

Figure **43** Front drop to back drop

the landing is almost exactly a vertical descent to the bed with only just enough rotation to ensure a horizontal position on contact with the bed. The stomach and leg muscles must be held tight to prevent the legs from collapsing downwards on landing. The position shown in Figure 44a, with the lower legs fairly high but with sufficient projection beyond the seat to give enough eccentricity to produce rotation, will, if adopted, enable the pupil to rebound and rotate to feet easily without any further positive action. Tension must be present in the body and legs before the landing on the back.

Figure 44b shows the pupil just clear of the bed and rotating forward, with the body still in almost the same position as for the landing. In Figure 44c the body is tucked just a little to increase the amount of rotation, needed to get around to the stomach. Before progressing to the whole move, practise producing a high rise to the feet from the back landing so that there is a certain amount of drop to the foot landing with the body well straightened. This ensures that there is enough space to complete the whole move. Then try the whole move. From the tucked position (Figure 44c) the body is opened out (Figure 44d) to decrease the rotation and prepare for the landing (Figure 44e).

At first it is difficult for pupils to realise that the slight forward setting of the legs coupled with the tension of the body is enough to ensure rotation. Each pupil will have to find the best personal placing of the legs. To increase height, a strong upward kick on landing on the back will make a considerable difference to the height of the rebound. This will be needed for further rotation.

Cradle (Early Twist)

Mastery of the back drop to front drop is the key to success in learning the cradle. The most useful one to learn is the early twisting cradle since it is a preliminary skill leading to the corkscrew ($1\frac{1}{2}$ twists), the Rob Roy ($2\frac{1}{2}$ twists) and the baby fliffus (cradle back or cradle overturned to back somersault).

From the back drop landing, shown in Figure 45a, kick vigorously up so that the tense body can rise straight, initiating twist by lifting the left shoulder whilst still in contact with the bed. Figure 45c shows the body starting to twist to the right. Leaving the arms outstretched keeps the speed of twist slow so that the eyes can watch the bed during the whole movement. The half twist is completed just after the highest point of the flight is reached (Figures 45d–e). The body is tucked very slightly (Figure 45f) to speed up the rotation to back drop and to help slow up the twist even more. Figure 45g shows the body in a good landing position ready to repeat the cradle or to rebound up to the feet.

The main problem is not having developed enough rotational power through the leg kick to achieve a high easy flight with enough room between the feet and the bed to avoid having to bend the legs.

Figure **44** Back drop to front drop

Figure **45** The cradle

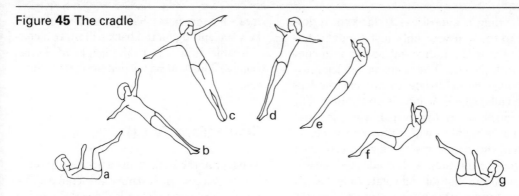

Cradle (Late Twist)

The cradle with late twist (Figures 46a–e) shows an easier but less useful way of completing the move. A vigorous up and under kick is still necessary, but the body is allowed to complete about three-quarters of the flight before any twist is produced by sweeping the left arm across the slightly piked body (RMI twisting) so that the half twist is completed in the last quarter of the movement. This can be practised at first by performing seat drop to front until easily accomplished and putting the half twist in just before landing.

Corkscrew (Back Drop, One and a Half Twists Forwards to Back Drop)

The corkscrew, or back drop one and a half twists forward to back drop, is a skilled move which, though not particularly difficult, gives a good sense of skilled performance. A cradle with arms wide is a good starting move to practise in order to get the idea of a powerful twist at the start of the move with the possibility of acceleration to complete more twist. Figure 47a shows the landing ready to kick the legs up for height and the arms held in a strong starting position. Figures 47b and

Figure **46** The cradle with late twist

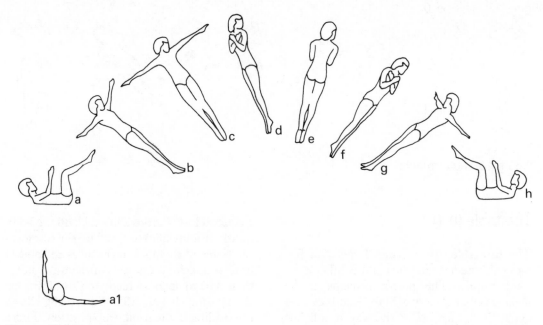

Figure **47** The corkscrew

c show the body having left the bed, the trunk straight and firm and the arms well out sideways from the body. This position is most important. Unless there is good tension right from the start and a good back drop to front drop rotation set up the performer will find that it is difficult to complete the one and a half twists easily before a landing is made. The arm position on landing is also very important. The arms should be held with the upper arm out sideways from the body and the forearms held almost vertical to the bed at the moment of impact. In this way it is easy to keep control of the arms as the rebound is made and the twist is initiated. If the arms are held too high, about head height, as the landing is made, they will tend to carry on moving in a direction which will take them above the head as rebound occurs. If they are held too low they will collapse on to the bed as the landing is made and it will be difficult to initiate the twist.

In order to initiate the twist, which is shown in Figure 47a1, the left shoulder is lifted on contact with the bed, the arms are held wide and the trunk muscles are tensed so that any twisting force put in is not lost in the loose segments of the body. Figures 47d, e and f show the arms pulled close into the chest, giving a very fast acceleration, to provide just over a full twist. The arms are opened out (Figure 47g) to slow down the twisting speed for the landing (Figure 47h). One of the main problems in this skill is a lack of rotation from back drop to front drop, so that the body is dropping down to the bed before the twist is finished. The performer must practise back drop to front drop straight as well as the twisting skill.

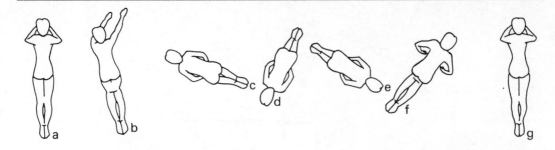

Figure **48** The turntable

Turntable (0.4)

The turntable can be considered as a fun move although it can prove quite difficult for some pupils. The problem seems to be making the whole move. Many pupils can get about three-quarters of the way round but then run out of space. There is also a tendency to roll over sideways a little through pushing too hard on one hand.

In Figure 48a the pupil has landed in the front drop position and is ready to push to the left by extending the arms against the bed to the right. It is important not to push down but to push to the side. Keep pushing until contact is lost (Figure 48b), tuck up the body tightly (Figure 48c) to speed up the sideways rotation and stay tucked (Figures 48d and e) until about three-quarters of the way round, then start to open up ready to slow down for the landing (Figure 48f). Figure 48g shows the landing in the front drop position. There is a tendency to open from the tuck too soon, slowing the twist enough to prevent a complete 360° sideways rotation. Any downwards push on the hands will tend to cause the top of the body to rise or roll over. When this happens the pupil tends to give up. Keep the head low when pushing sideways on the bed.

3

Introduction to Somersault Rotation (Including Side Somersaults)

Hands and Knees Drop, Forward Turnover to Back Drop

With a low jump and take-off, as shown in Figure 49a, drop into the hands and knees landing position (Figure 49b). On landing push down on the feet or lift the buttocks, without bending the arms or lowering the head (see Figure 49c). A slight forward push on the hands should enable the body to rise up without travel whilst the head is fixed in such a position to keep the bed in view as the body rises and rotates, until the position shown in Figure 49e is reached. The head is then dropped, the rotation speeds up a little and the back drops down on to the bed and vision is regained (Figure 49f). This move is a relatively easy way of approaching the first attempts at turning the head under. Note that the rotation is initiated either by pushing down on the feet or by lifting the hips, causing the bed to be depressed, and then the return of the bed lifts the hips and legs upwards. Rotation is not inititated by dropping the head or by letting the arms bend so that the top of the body drops down. Dropping the head and pushing down on the legs are both examples of the application of eccentric force. Pushing down on the legs gives height; dropping the head cuts the height.

Hands and Knees Drop, Forward Turnover Tucked to Seat Drop

This move is designed to help progress the pupil from the turnover to back and to give practice in tucking up to increase the speed of rotation so that the pupil lands on the seat.

All the techniques are the same until you

Figure **49** Hands and knees drop forward turn over to back drop

are in the position shown in Figure 50a. At this point the body is tucked up tightly (Figure 50b). Once this position is attained the

can be easily performed without travel. Any forward lean on the first landing will result in travel, and dropping of the head will result in loss of height and some loss of orientation. The longer the bed is in sight, the more relaxedly the pupil will perform.

Although support is not normally needed the very nervous or less skilled pupil might well respond better with some support. Support is described on p. 66 (Figure 75a–e).

Figure **50** Hands and knees drop forward turn over tucked to seat drop

body is quickly opened up to the position shown in Figure 50c. This will slow the body up so that a landing can be made in the seat drop position shown in Figure 50d. This practice enables the pupil to get the feel of slowing down and speeding up in flight just as in the complete somersault. As a progression it has the advantage of being performed low so that the landing is not heavy. Support is not normally needed. Practise this until it

Tucked Front Somersault to Seat Drop (0.4)

The tucked front somersault to seat drop may be used as the last of the progressions before the pupil attempts the whole move to feet. It is useful as a control move since it requires a gentle rotation to effect a good landing and, since the trunk is vertical on

Figure **51** Tucked front somersault to seat drop

landing, it is almost the same in rotation as the complete move, but it feels different and the performer has consciously to take-off more gently. Figures 51a–d show the take-off and tuck as for the tucked front somersault, but the rotation is a little slower and the pupil is not so far round in the rotation. Figure 51e shows the point where the tucked position is about to be opened up. The hands are released and the legs straightened out to the piked position (Figures 51f and g). The speed of rotation is decreased, but not so much as when the pupil opens the body to the straight position. The final descent is made to the sitting position with the hands in the correct position pointing forwards (Figures 51h and i). If this can be achieved constantly, and easily, a little more power at take-off will make the tucked front somersault to feet more easily performed.

Front Somersault Tucked (0.4)

The front somersault tucked is usually one of the first somersaults to be learned. It is a much more natural movement than the back somersault and can be easily visualised from the normal agility skills learned in any school.

A very important part of the front somersault tucked is the use of the correct arm swing. Figure 52a shows the arms held behind the body at the start of the jump. They are swung forwards and upward as the legs are straightened and the hips kept in a slightly rearwards displaced position. This displacement of the hips should not be too great or it will lead to the head dropping. Additionally the arms should not be held up in the air in front of the body as the start is made or the whole move will be pulled down. Many coaches see the pulled down arm action as suitable since it seems to give easy natural rotation. It does give easy rotation, but it also tends to cause low, travelling, unsighted starts to any forward somersaulting skill, making a good upward lift and a powerful rotation very difficult. A well performed front somersault should be well sighted throughout most of its course.

Figure 52b shows the pupil just after take-off, when the body is still only slightly piked and rising. Figure 52c shows the tuck just

Figure **52** Front somersault tucked

starting, indicating that the start is well phased. Figure 52d and e show the tuck with the legs grasped just below the knees, the head turning down towards the chest and the opening just beginning. Figures 52f and g show the body opened right out to a straight position with the rotation slowed down, the arms getting ready for the landing, and Figure 52h shows the landing with the forward rotation just stopped and the arms ready for the next take-off. Note the phasing, showing an easy, well open start, a good tuck for acceleration and quite an early opening slowing down the rotation enough to avoid over rotation.

Front Somersault Piked (0.5)

The front somersault piked is not very difficult to perform once the front somersault tucked has been mastered. There is however a tendency for the performer to pull the move down instead of lifting up at take-off.

In order to avoid this the arms should be well lifted and an attempt to keep the body straight for a short time after take-off should be made. If this is carried out the move will be well phased and will show an initial flight, a good sharp pike, and an early opening for the landing. If there is not an attempt to get a lifted straight take-off, the move will have the appearance of a low hurried somersault with the pike beginning almost at take-off. As in the piked back somersault the hands should grasp the legs at, or below, the knees. The forearms can be placed along the thigh to give a good line or hands should grasp low down towards the ankles to give a good sharp angle to the pike. *See* Figures 53a–d showing the ankle grasp and the phased take-off. Some pupils may not be able to pike sharply but they can still keep the move tidy by putting their arms well in line with the legs even if the grasp is not low. Working on a phased piked front drop will help the pupil to appreciate the type of take-off that is required. *See* section on piked front drop (p. 30).

Figure **53** Front somersault piked showing the ankle grasp and the phased take-off

Front Somersault Straight (0.5)

The front somersault straight is a move that is not very often seen and is probably considered interesting but not very useful. It can be a very good practice for the barani, after the barani has been learned in the normal way to get over to the pupil the idea of a straight lift into the air, thus avoiding the problem of pulling down into the bed. The double front straight with half twist has now been successfully performed and the basic practice will be the front somersault straight, the one and three-quarter front somersault straight, and finally the fliffus. The main problem causing difficulties with the front somersault straight is the common one of dropping the head at take-off.

It is essential, at the start of the move, to lift the arms strongly upwards and to hold the head up. This helps to avoid any tendency to lean forwards, or to drop the head at the last instant before take-off, and lose height (Figures 54a and b). The pupil should then try to watch the bed after take-off until it disappears as the somersault progresses past 180° (Figures 54c–e). If vision is not held to this point, there is a tendency to fold the head down a little and to let the body pike, thus losing the straight position. The take-off is, of course, more powerful than for a tucked or piked front somersault. As the descent to the bed begins (Figure 54f), vision should be re-established quickly by inclining the head forwards a little without losing the straight body (Figures 54g–i). This move has a nice slow-motion feel. It does not take many attempts to get the idea of the straight lift.

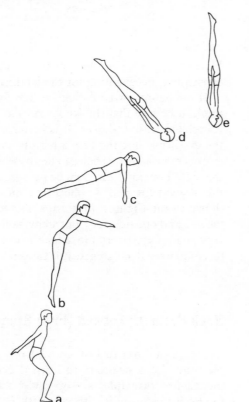

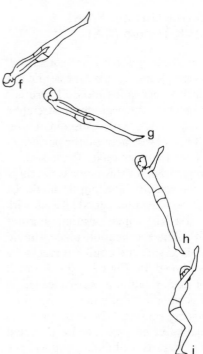

Figure **54** Front somersault straight

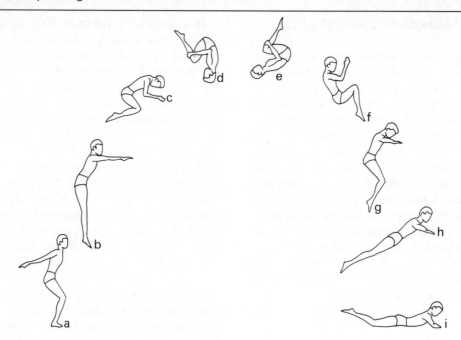

Figure **55** One and one quarter front somersault tucked

One and One Quarter Front Somersault Tucked (0.5)

The one and one quarter front somersault tucked is a simple move, as is the one and one quarter back somersault tucked. There is a tendency again for the beginner to attempt a low fast somersault, with consequent over rotation. This may be because the performer is anxious not to under rotate the move.

The preparation for this move is the tucked front somersault. The pupil should be expected to be able to get a good take-off with the body in a fairly open position (Figures 55a and b). The acceleration phase should only take place after the pupil has reached a height as shown in Figure 55c. A small amount of extra rotation power is needed so that there is an opportunity to open out for a slowly rotating landing. The extra power is used to enable the performer to have rotated as shown in Figures 55d and e, and to have the body at the normal angle for a foot landing when well above the bed (Figure 55f).

Figures 55g–i show the opening out and consequent deceleration for the landing.

It can be somewhat difficult at first for the pupil to believe that the whole move can be completed without hurry. It is better to use the crash mat for the first attempts so that any over or under rotation can be absorbed in the mat. The pupil can then be persuaded to use a good lift and to phase the move as shown in the Figures. Performed as shown, the one and one quarter front somersault is a very good preparatory move for the one and three-quarter front somersault tucked.

Back Pullover Tucked (First Stages)

The back pullover tucked is a relatively simple move for a beginner to learn if certain mechanical principles are observed during the performance of it with very little height. It uses a slightly off-balance landing, a backward roll and then a slight rebound.

In Figure 56a, the pupil is standing in a slightly crouched position ready to take off. The arms are raised and the hands are placed one at each side of the head for support in case of a bad landing. With a gentle downward push into the bed the pupil drops on to the bed making sure that the seat lands where the feet were before the take off (Figures 56b and c). Notice in Figure 56c, there is slight backward lean so that the body will roll backwards along the bed after the landing on the end of the spine. If this is allowed to happen and then the knees are tucked into the chest, the body will roll up on to the shoulders. The rebound of the bed will coincide with this

Figure **56** Back pullover tucked

and there will be enough clearance for the head to come through allowing the pupil to turn over on to the feet (Figures 56d–e).

It is important that the pupil does not drop on to the bed with any backward travel along the bed. This will cause a forward reactive return rebound which will make the correct performance of the move very difficult. Very little height is needed to perform this move, provided the pupil does not throw the shoulders backwards as the seat comes into contact. It is very easy to perform and is useful in helping to convince pupils that

correct techniques help to make simple skills easy. Later it is easy to move on to the type of back pullover that uses the upward leg kick with the flat back landing.

Back Pullover (Bomb Type)

The 'Bomb' type back pullover is for the talented pupil only to attempt as an introduction to back pullover type moves. The pupil drops about 18–24 inches on to the lower end of the spine with a slight backward lean. The hands are holding the shins just below the knees. As soon as a contact is made the hands pull the lower legs into a tighter tuck and the body should spin easily round backwards until the bed is sighted and the legs released for a landing. Figures 57a–h illustrate the sequence of events. It is most important that the landing is made with the slight backward tilt so that backward rotation is initiated, and that the tuck is pulled on impact so that the rotation is accelerated.

As a first stage the pupil can squat at the front of the trampoline bed holding on to the edge of the bed with the body at a slight backward angle. On releasing the grip on the bed the body will automatically roll backwards (see Figures 57c, d). It is not wise to allow the pupil to throw the head back since this leads to excessive travel along the bed and may impair rotation so that the pupil

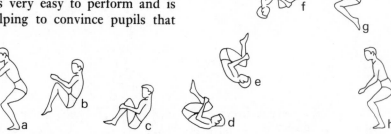

Figure **57** Back pullover (bomb type)

lands short or even on the head. Having found that the body will roll easily, the pupil can make a low and easy drop on to the end of the spine, landing with the back rounded and the hands held up on either side of the head as for the backward roll on the floor (*see* Figures 56b–d). As soon as contact is made with the bed the knees should be pulled into the chest. This action will round the back even more, so that the body rolls round and the rebound occurs just as the shoulders come into contact with the bed. The body is then lifted clear of the bed as the head comes round. If there is very little rotation or height the hands can be used to support the body as the head passes under the body. This makes it a very safe practice, and it can get the pupil used to backward rotation. It also shows the pupil how little effort is needed to be able to turn over. The main problem comes from trying to initiate rotation by throwing the head and shoulders back. If this is tried there is usually a distinct lack of rotation or the chance of the pupil landing on the top of the head. It can be seen from Figure 57d that, if the shoulders hit the bed first, there is an equal and opposite force from the bed pushing the shoulders back in the direction from which they came. This effectively stops most of the rotational force.

Back Pullover to Stomach

The back pullover to stomach is a useful progression for the three-quarter back somersault. From a standard stance and take-off (Figures 58a and b), the pupil drops on to the back with the legs bent ready for an upward kick (Figures 58c and d). Having made the upward kick with the lower legs the body is stretched as rotation occurs, thus slowing down the body to prepare for a stomach landing (Figures 58e–h). It is important that the stretch is carried out as the body rises or over rotation will occur.

At first it may be easier to pass through a handstand position since the move can be carried out with only a little height. The contact with the hands helps to slow up any extra rotation and also helps to judge the landing on the stomach.

For extra practice the pupil can pull through and then repeat the move again and again. This will then give plenty of practice in the three-quarter back rotation to stomach.

Back Pullover to Feet with Leg Kick

The most useful type of back pullover is performed by landing with the back flat, but with the lower back being very slightly before the rest of the back. The legs are held with the thighs at approximately right-angles to the bed (Figure 59a). On contact with the bed the

Figure **58** Back pullover to stomach

Figure **59** Back pullover to feet with leg kick

lower leg is kicked smartly upwards. This will give a downwards reaction at the lower end of the back and the body will rotate backwards as it rises out of the bed (Figure 59b). A tucking up of the body (Figure 59c) will increase the speed of rotation so that the body will go round further. The body is opened out again (Figure 59d) for a landing on the feet (Figure 59e).

It is important on the first landing not to pull the legs in closer to the chest since this will result in slower rotation and more travel due to the altered angle of push into the bed. The arms can be held around the legs below the knees to help stabilise the legs for the kick.

Back Somersault Tucked (0.4)

WARNING: THIS MOVE SHOULD ONLY BE ATTEMPTED WITH THE SUPERVISION OF A COACH, USING PROPER SUPPORTS AND POSSIBLY A CRASH MAT.

Make sure that the back pullover and the back drop have been mastered. This will give experience of backward rotation and acceleration and looking for the bed on landing. From a balanced start (Figure 60a) swing the arms powerfully forwards and upwards, at the same time displacing the hips forwards. This is the same as for the back drop but

Figure **60** Back somersault tucked

much more powerful (Figure 6ob). Make sure that the head is not dropped back or forward at the take-off. After take-off, tuck up as in Figure 6oc. If you have kept the head in line it will then appear to have been taken forward. As soon as you have rotated over the top (Figure 6oe) start to open out and to look for the bed (Figure 6of), straighten out the body to slow up the rotation ready for the landing and swing the arms gently into place for the next take-off (Figures 6og and h).

It is essential that there be no lean or travel will occur. This may cause the pupil to reduce the leg push to avoid travel. This, in turn, may lead to loss of somersault rotation power and thus danger of falling on the head. It is essential that work on this move is undertaken very carefully. Always work with a coach, and not other pupils, until the skill of the back somersault is mastered. Discuss your problems, seek support, and make sure that you do not try the move out on your own. Proper progressions will lead to success. Go back a stage if you have a problem. Use the above information together with your coach.

Back Somersault Piked (0.5)

For most pupils an easy approach to this move is by gradually straightening the legs at the knees in the tucked back somersault. This enables the pupil to go by easy stages from a move that is known to one which is not. The main problem with the piked somersault is the phasing. There is a tendency to pike immediately after take-off, which is a little early. The pupil should aim to get a good take-off without lean or tipping back of the head and then, when the straight take-off position has been shown, to fold quickly at the waist with the legs straight at the knees and hands along the line of the calf, preferably below the knee to help the line of the legs.

Support can be given by the coach in the first stages, mainly to avoid any tendency by the pupil to lean back and to help give the confidence to wait a little longer before folding for the pike. The coach can use the hand or can place it in the middle of the shoulders

Figure **61** Back somersault piked

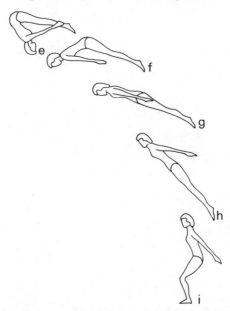

to help the forward and upward lift of the chest. The arms' swing is as for the layout back and the legs also should move in the forward direction as for the layout and tuck back somersaults. The pupil should be looking at the shins in mid-flight.

Figures 61a–i show the phasing. Note: in Figure 61b the body is still straight–piking should not begin until well after take-off.

Back Somersault Straight (0.5)

This move is easier to learn than the back somersault tucked, but there is a strong tendency to get the rotation by swinging the head back and doing a low fast somersault with a very arched back. This practice must be avoided and the move approached in such a way that the back is as straight as possible, and the head is in line with the body and only tipped back to get an early sight of the bed for landing (Figures 62b–d).

In order to avoid the above problems, it can first be performed with support. The support is not necessary for safe performance of the somersault but to enable the pupil to lift the chest, to keep the head in line and to gain a reasonable height. For the pupil a powerful forward lift of the arms, held straight (Figure 62c) and stopped at approximately shoulder height, helps the lift and helps to avoid backward lean. Letting the arms lift higher may help the lift, but for those pupils who do not have a powerful abdominal section, some backward lean may be the result.

Figure **62** Back somersault straight

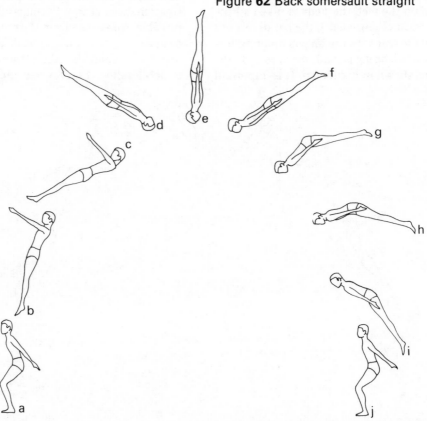

The arms can be brought into the sides as soon as the take-off is completed. A slight piking at the end will bring the performer into position for a landing (Figures 62g and h). There should be a definite feeling that the legs are being lifted forwards without letting the body kink. Figures 62a–d show the arm action: try to keep the back as straight as possible, as shown in Figures 62b–d.

Back Somersault Tucked to Seat Drop (0.4)

The tucked back somersault to seat is one of the first progressions beyond the simple tucked back somersault to feet and does not involve the performer in any more rotation. Figures 63a–g show that the move is exactly the same. However, instead of just coming in to land on the feet, the body is piked a little at the waist (Figure 63h), the hands are put behind the seat with the fingers pointing forward and a landing is made on the seat in the position shown in Figure 63i. It is important

to make sure that the hands are placed with the fingers pointing forward since the extra height makes the landing heavier than the normal seat drop. It is also important that the pupil does not put extra rotational power into the take-off, since this would result in a fast rotating seat drop landing which could result in a shoulder wrench.

Tucked One and One Quarter Back Somersault to Back Drop (0.5)

The one and one quarter back somersault tucked to back drop is an easy move to learn once the back somersault tucked has been mastered. The technique for this skill is not just to hold on to the tucked position until a landing is made but to try to put a little more rotational power into the take-off so that it is possible to open out from the tucked position to make a slowly rotating back landing. Figures 64a–d show the take-off and beginnings of acceleration. Figures 64e and f show the

Figure **63** Back somersault tucked to seat drop

acceleration completed and the trunk rotated until it is horizontal. Figure 64g shows the performer in a position with the trunk almost vertical which would enable a good foot landing to be made. However, the height from the bed ensures that rotation will carry on. Figure 64h indicates further deceleration and Figures 64i and j show the folding of the body for the back landing. This landing is of course ready for take-off from the back.

If the pupil merely hangs on to the tuck the body is usually rotating too fast and the landing is heavy and often high on the shoulders. This results in a crumpling of the body on impact and a consequent inability to get a controlled rebound from the back. Quite often the inexperienced coach will be content to allow the pupil to drop down on to the back still tucked, using a low fast somersault. It must be emphasised that this is incorrect and will impair further progress. It is not a good technique if the one and one quarter back is to be used as a preparation for the double back somersault.

Side Somersault (0.4)

The side somersault is not a competition move at present, but in time, in the search for originality and difficulty, it could well be included; there is no reason why it should not.

Figure 65a shows the starting position with the feet slightly apart, the body slightly bowed in the direction that the arms are held, ready to be displaced to the opposite side to set up sideways rotation.

Figure 65b shows the arms being swung vigorously to the right and the right leg being raised in the same direction as the hips are also displaced to the right. The final push into the bed with the left leg gives the last bit of rotational force to the body in the desired direction of rotation.

Figures 65c–e show the body in the tucked position to give acceleration to the body which is already rotating. Since it is just as easy to tuck up tight when rotating sideways as in a forwards or backwards direction, it is possible for double side somersaults to

Figure **64** Tucked one and one quarter back somersault to back drop

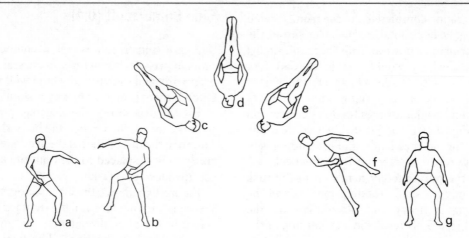

Figure **65** Side somersault

be performed after much practice at singles by a competent performer.

Figures 65f and g show the body in the open position now rotating slower ready to land. Notice that it is more likely that the performer will land with the legs slightly apart with one foot in front of the other, due to the sideways rotation of the body. Swing-time side somersaults can be performed with practice. There is a tendency for some performers to carry out this move as a slightly twisted back somersault.

4

Support Methods

General Principles

Without support from the coach, by use of the various methods now developed, the execution of many of the very complicated moves would not have been achieved by top trampolining performers. Nor would the ordinary participant have progressed so far in the learning of less complicated but still difficult and possibly dangerous moves. The combination of simple progressions, hand supports, crash mat landings, use of the rig for the first stages of double somersaults and twisting somersaults, combined with the use of two support methods simultaneously, has changed the learning opportunities for many pupils.

This section of the book covers the use of the crash mat, the rig and many hand support skills. It must be remembered that the use of support methods only helps learning and teaching: it does not replace the process. It means that the coach will have to learn the physical skills of supporting. These can be tiring and time-consuming and need experience. The good coach will have a wide selection of skills to use in order to lead the pupil from beginning stages SAFELY to expert performance at whatever level the pupil can manage. It is good practice also to teach supporting skills to the more experienced performers. More supporters are then available to increase participation, to help instil a sense of responsibility and involvement, and to prepare for the future development of pupils into coaches if they have that desire.

Use of the Crash Mat

One of the most useful developments in the safe teaching of trampolining was the introduction of the use of the crash mat on the bed of the trampoline. This avoids some of the many hard landings suffered by pupils when learning movements on the front or the back, when the angle of landing may be critical and any deviation prove to be uncomfortable or dangerous. Front and back landings are particularly difficult to support either with manual spotting or in the belt, since the extra distance the pupil falls causes a difficulty for the coach, who may not be able to bend low enough and still maintain a strong support or who may not be able to handle the extra length of rope needed and still give a safe support.

The crash mat is a foam pad covered in either cotton, plastic or plasticised nylon. It comes in various sizes ranging from approximately 6 feet by 4 feet by 8 inches to 10 feet by 4 feet by 1 foot. Obviously there is a considerable difference in weight and it is wise to purchase crash mats with an express purpose in mind. The large size mats are useful for placing at the ends of the trampolines in case any pupil lands on or near the end (*see* Figure 66a). The smaller mats are useful for pushing on to the bed just before the pupil lands to absorb the landing force and thus make the landing, if incorrect, more comfortable. Both coach and pupils must be skilled in the use of the mats. Practice must be given to those likely to be pushing the

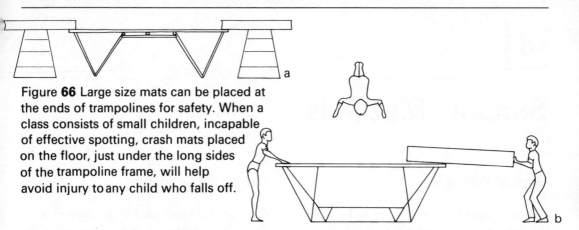

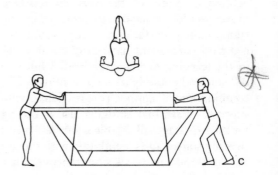

Figure **66** Large size mats can be placed at the ends of trampolines for safety. When a class consists of small children, incapable of effective spotting, crash mats placed on the floor, just under the long sides of the trampoline frame, will help avoid injury to any child who falls off.

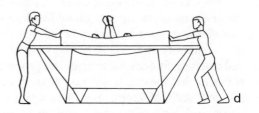

mats on before any pupil makes any attempt at a potentially dangerous move.

It is important also to get the pupil used to the idea of the mat being pushed in underneath him whilst on the way down for the landing (*See* Figure 66b–d). This can be practised with a simple move like the seat drop so that there is no problem if the pushers do not get it quite right. There should normally be two people to push the mat on to the bed and for added safety there should be two people on the other side of the trampoline with arms outstretched just in case the mat is pushed too far across the bed. Progress from simple moves to more difficult moves, so that the mat pushers become more and more experienced, getting ready for the bigger moves for which the mat is really necessary. It must always be remembered that the crash mat does not do away with the need for proper coaching. The mat is there just in case a mistake is made and also to enable the pupil to work on build-up skills, which may have a back or front landing and which might be a problem to handle, if done with over or under rotation.

The crash mat is especially useful for fairly basic moves like the front drop, full twist to front drop, crash dive and three-quarter back somersault. It is even possible to jump on the mat for the above moves since they are not dependent on a great deal of height for success. Of course jumping on the crash mat does kill the rebound of the bed. This however does not really matter in the beginning stages. After some successful attempts have been made progress can be made to taking off from the bed and then having the mat pushed in for the landing.

The mat can be used in conjunction with the rig for moves such as the one and three-quarter front somersault, one and three-quarter back somersault, two and three-quarter front somersault, full in one and three-quarter front somersault, half in one and three-quarter front somersault and any fliffus build-up where a front or back landing at the one and three-quarter somersault stage could be a big problem if there is a failure to make the correct amount of rotation.

It may also be good sense to use the crash mat for the first attempts out of the belt for moves such as the double back, barani out and in and any move where the performer is likely to fall short or over rotate. There is no doubt that the use of the crash mat gives the pupil a feeling of security when about to take-off for a difficult move. The effects of the impact are reduced and the rebound is made less powerful. The pupil knows that the landing will be more comfortable. It must be realised too that the removal of the mat will possibly also cause the pupil to feel less confident at take-off, since a spoiled move can now result in a painful landing. It is now necessary to make sure that the time for the removal of the mat is carefully considered by both coach and pupil. A fall at this stage can cause injury or loss of confidence or can cause a major setback in the learning process. The judgement of the coach as to the readiness of the pupil is required. All factors must be taken into account and a properly considered decision taken. It may be necessary for some time to start the pupil on the mat for a couple of attempts and then progress to some attempts without the mat. This sequence may operate for some training sessions until the pupil is able to dispense with the mat altogether. A small loss of confidence may cause the pupil to ask for the mat again. Do not deny this use: it will usually not last for long. It may make all the difference between progress or a position of potential stalemate. However, the coach will have to draw on experience to try to make the best decision in each case.

Spotters

Spotters are an essential part of trampolining: they provide safety for participants. They are themselves participants, who either have taken their turn or are waiting to do so.

Figure 66c (*see* page 58) shows the stance adopted by a spotter. One leg is forward and one braced back to take the force of any performer who may be moving towards the end or the side of the frame. The arms should be rested upon the frame in a state of alertness. If a performer should need support the spotter should push towards the performer as shown in Figure 65b (right) or higher if necessary. The fact that a spotter is present does give some confidence to the performer. The spotter can also encourage and coach the performer at some levels. The spotter does not replace the teacher and is not in charge.

Checking the Rig

It is important to check the rig before use, both the twisting belt and the ordinary somersaulting belt. Figure 67a shows the twisting belt unfastened. Looking at the performer from the front, it shows the chrome adjusting bars on the left and the fastening hook on the right.

Figure 67b shows the belt closed with the hook over the appropriate bar on the chrome ladder. There is also a safety spigot on the inner part of the hook side of the belt (Figure 67c). This spigot is designed to fit over one of the chrome bars to avoid the belt undoing as the outer sliding belt is tightened. The belt is closed and locked by pushing the chrome ladder end of the belt towards your stomach whilst at the same time pulling the hook end to your right until the locking spigot engages.

Figure 67e shows the outer belt of the twisting belt. It revolves in the inner section and should be tightened only so far that it

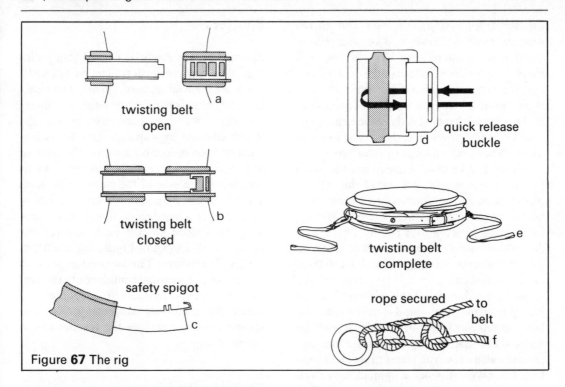

twisting belt
open

a

quick release
buckle

d

twisting belt
closed

b

twisting belt
complete

e

safety spigot

c

rope secured
to
belt

f

Figure **67** The rig

will not come out of the lip of the inner belt.

Figure 67d shows the quick release buckle of the somersaulting belt: the black arrow shows the positioning and the direction of the belt through the buckle. It is tightened by pulling in the direction of the arrow until secure and not able to slip upwards. The tag on the buckle is pulled in the opposite direction to release the tension immediately.

Checks

[a] The straps for wear and broken stitches or rivets.

[b] The twisting action of the belt for free running whilst still secure.

[c] The 'D' rings or circles to see they are not catching.

[d] The tying of the ropes to the nylon straps or rings.

[e] The weight of the pupil before starting to support a skill.

Using the Rig

The rig or safety harness is a very important piece of equipment for the pupil and the teacher of trampolining. To use it skilfully a good deal of practice is needed. Figure 68a shows the coach holding the rig ready to start. One hand holds the rope, which is wrapped round the hand at face height or just below. The other hand is held above this hand, making sure that at least the thumb and forefinger are encircling the rope. In this way, at all times, the rope is held under the control of both hands. Test the correctness of the grasp by getting the pupil to perform a seat drop. If the rope is the correct length the pupil will be able to drop down without the coach having his/her arm pulled out of its socket. Put the rope under enough tension to

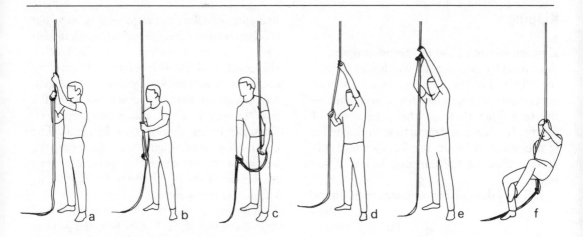

Figure **68** Using the rig

make sure that it is not flapping about loosely or too tight to allow the pupil to descend into the bed. Having checked the grip on the rope, practise with the pupil jumping low.

Set the tension and ask the pupil to begin. The rope will first go up a little way as the pupil sinks into the bed on making the first movement, then you will pull the rope down as the pupil goes up into the air. Keep the tension and remember to hold the rope down at the bottom of the travel (Figure 68b) until the pupil begins to descend. The descent of the pupil will then pull your hand up. Do not try to move the rope upwards to co-ordinate with the descent of the pupil since there is a tendency to move too fast and to let the rope go slack. The reason for holding the rope still at the bottom of the pull is that, at the top of the jump, there is a short period of time when there is no movement either up or down. Figure 68c shows the procedure when the pupil is capable of jumping high. The rope will travel a considerable distance down towards the floor. The second hand, which is held higher than the one around which the rope is wrapped, allows the rope to slide through until the bottom hand has reached the end of the travel and then pulls the rope down.

As the pupil sinks into the bed the upper hand rises first (Figure 68d) and is followed by the hand around which the rope is wrapped (Figure 68e). The whole sequence then is right hand down, followed by left hand, pause at the bottom, left hand up followed by right hand pause at the top. Enough downward pull must be kept on the rope to ensure that it is just taut the whole time, neither giving the pupil too much lift nor preventing a full descent into the bed.

Figure 68f shows the supporter taking the strain of a heavy descent from height. When the pupil is about to descend, and the coach knows that a lot of support is going to be needed, the right hand is placed under the seat with the hand clamped against the body and the coach's whole weight is put in to the hand and rope. This method will stop the rope rushing through the hands and burning the skin.

It must be emphasised that it takes time and skill to use the harness well. The coach should practise at all levels to gain the necessary skill since the pupil might at some time need all the coach's skill if there is an emergency stop to be made. The main fault of those learning to use the rig is to let the rope get too slack. This can distract the pupil and cause a time delay in the application of the braking effect.

Kipping

Kipping is one of the advanced supporting skills used by experienced coaches to control the rebound of the bed so that a pupil can concentrate, during a learning stage, more on the technique than on the production of height. If a coach is supporting on the bed it is necessary to be on the bed without adversely affecting the jumping action of the pupil.

It is very difficult for the coach to be on the

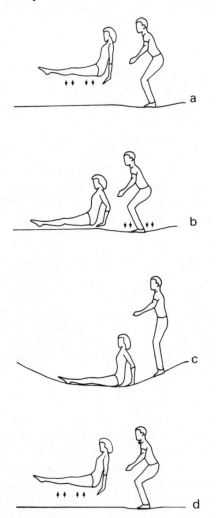

Figure **69** Kipping

bed and not affect the pupil in any way, but it is better to enhance performance than hinder it. The main problem seems to be that the coach and pupil cannot work together consistently and thus the pupil does not gain any advantage from the coach being on the bed. However if the coach can 'kip' well there can be an advantage to the pupil. The coach can give extra height, can help keep the height of the jumps consistent or can keep the height of the pupil down if necessary by killing the bed a little.

'Kipping' to give extra height is illustrated in Figures 69a–d. In Figure 69a, the pupil is descending towards the bed and the coach is standing in a ready position with the legs bent ready for the push down of the bed. For the less experienced coach it is important to stand with the legs bent so that the exact timing of the push is not missed. Figure 69b shows the pupil just landing and the coach pushing the bed down quickly to catch the speed of descent of the pupil. Figure 69c shows the full depression of the bed by both the weight of the pupil and the weight and push of the coach.

Figure 69d shows the pupil rising up into the air: the coach has bent legs which have effectively removed most of his weight from the bed, giving the stored energy of both the coach's and pupil's depression of the bed to the pupil. The more skilled the coach the more effective the efficient storage of energy. Getting it just right needs practice and experience.

Many beginners stand with straight legs as the pupil is landing, bending the legs as the bed is depressed instead of straightening them, and then straightening them as the bed rises up again. This gives the opposite effect from kipping and 'kills' the bed. This 'mistake' can be used to kill the bed effectively when standing in for the landing of a pupil from a movement that they are learning, and is also one of the skills of the experienced coach.

Hand Holds for Supporting

The two hand holds shown in Figures 70a and b are designed to give a comfortable but secure hand hold by the supporter on the pupil. In both holds the thumb and forefinger of the supporter are around the wrist of the pupil, palms are together and the thumb of the pupil is between the second and third fingers of the supporter's hand (*see* Figure 70a), which is the support for the front somersault and other forward moves. The supporter's hand is underneath the pupil's hand.

Figure 70b shows the hold for the back somersault. The grip is exactly the same and will, when the pupil has completed a front somersault or forward roll, be automatic. The pupil holds up the left hand at about shoulder height with the palm to the front. The supporter then places the right hand across the pupil's hand as shown in the figure. At the end of the back somersault the hand hold will be ready for the front somersault. Thus the pupil will be able to perform a front somersault followed by a back somersault or a back somersault followed by a front somersault without changing the starting hand hold. A back somersault followed by a barani will also be possible.

If the pupil is an adult male with a large hand it is sometimes better to place the pupil's thumb between the supporter's third and fourth fingers instead of the second and third.

Front Drop Support

In addition to the selection of progressions for learning the front drop, some manual support may be given to the pupil who is still nervous enough about the move to be failing in most attempts at a proper take-off.

Figure 71a shows the ordinary front somersault support, pupil's left hand supported by the supporter's right hand. Figure 71b shows the supporter's hand on the front upper part of the pupil's chest.

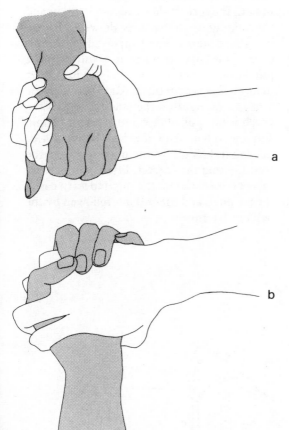

a

b

Figure **70** Hand holds for supporting

a

b

Figure **71** Manual support

Both methods are used to try to get the pupil to lift up for the take-off and then to give support and reassurance at the top of the lift and to guide the descent to the bed or crash mat. Care must be taken to see that the release is at the right moment in the descent so that the pupil is still under control, is horizontal, and can land in the same position.

After some practice it is usual to find that the support can be lessened and the hand removed soon after take-off. Be ready to give stronger support if the pupil shows nervousness again. Do not insist too strongly that the pupil relinquishes support, rather leave it to the pupil to suggest a lessening.

Back Drop Support

Two forms of back drop support may be used for those pupils who find the move difficult to carry out in the correct manner. Figures 72a and b show the stance taken by the coach when placing the hand on the back of the pupil in order to help avoid a strong backward push with the shoulders. The object of the support is to guide the pupil's shoulders in a vertical direction as the take-off is made so that the pupil gets the feeling of the correct direction and the resultant slow rotation to the back drop landing.

The alternative support is used if the pupil has not got a very strong backward push at

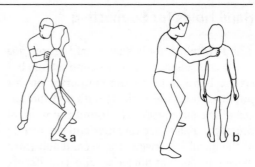

Figure **72** Back drop support: method 1

take-off but does need a little encouragement to move in the right direction. Figure 73a shows the hand hold as used for the front somersault. Lifting the pupil's hand forward and upward encourages the correct action at lift-off, the correct slow rotation in flight and the landing on the back as shown in Figure 76a at the start of the supported back pull-over. This support up to feet will help the pupil to get the correct action from back drop to feet if this is a problem. Make sure that the arms are straight on the landing so that the coach is not pulled down towards the pupil, and the rebound of the bed is not killed, making it difficult for the pupil to rise to the feet. Getting the correct, lifted, straight rise to feet is essential for the pupil to learn easily the porpoise and the ball out followed by the ball out barani.

Figure **73** Half twist to back drop with support

Half Twist to Back Drop with Support

It is important that the half twist to back drop is learned in such a way that the pupil is not leaning forward or swinging the legs round in an arc. To help this the supporter takes the hold shown in Figure 73a. This is the standard hold for the front somersault. The supporter is holding the pupil's left hand with the left hand. The pupil's hand is lifted so that it is up near the shoulder, to induce a lifted shoulder instead of a dropped shoulder. The pupil has to produce the twist whilst the supporter helps him to avoid dropping of the head and shoulders. Figure 73b shows the pupil just after take-off with the body straight, the gaze on the bed just ahead of the cross, or actually at the cross, and the legs pushed in a backwards direction.

In Figure 73c the pupil still has the gaze on the bed as the descent is made, only turning the head as the landing is about to be made. Figure 73d shows the pupil about to land, with the head turned to line up with the body looking down at the bed, as it were, through the body. The legs are also bent for the landing. The supporter is not there to pull the pupil round in the turn but only to give reassurance about positioning at take-off in flight and on landing.

Full Twist to Back Drop with Support

The support position for this move is the same as for the half twist to crash dive and the back somersault with full twist. It is shown in Figure 74a. The pupil should start with a slight turn in the direction of twist for the first few attempts, turning the head to sight the bed. Supporter's right hand will hold the left hand of the pupil behind the pupil's back. Supporter's left hand will be on the pupil's left shoulder. This can be used to indicate to the pupil when the twist should be started, rather than to pull the pupil round into the twist.

Figure 74b shows the pupil just after take-off, watching the bed and pushing the legs forwards along the bed, keeping the body stretched. The right arm of the pupil is held wide (Figures 74b and c) as the twist moves round to about the half-way stage.

Figures 74d and e show the arms of the pupil brought in to accelerate the twist at the same time as the hand held by the supporter is brought across the body, so that both arms are in the position of least resistance to the twist. Figure 74f shows the pupil about to land in the same position as for the half twist to back drop shown in Figure 74f.

Use of this support will help the pupil to keep calm and not to rush the twist or to fling the arms in a wide arc across the trampoline bed through thinking that the amount of twist needed was very high. As the pupil comes to perform the move easily, gradually relinquish the support until it is performed unaided.

Figure **74** Full twist to back drop with support

Figure **75** Back drop half twist to feet and full twist to feet

Back Drop, Half Twist to Feet and Full Twist to Feet

A good back drop half twist to feet often proves quite a difficult skill to many pupils. The key is initiating the twist on contact with the bed and keeping a very strong tension in the mid section of the body and in the legs. Support may help the pupil to succeed.

Figure 75a shows the pupil in the back landing position and the supporter with legs well splayed holding the straight left arm of the pupil. On contact with the bed the coach will have to give a slight kip to the pupil from the low stance shown. Instruct the pupil not to bend the left arm and pull in order to turn, but to use it as a form of stabiliser making the wide arm turn a little easier to achieve. Figure 75b shows the pupil after leaving the bed with the right arm held wide.

It is fairly straightforward to progress from the half twist to the full twist simply by bringing the right arm in to the body. The supporter has to let the holding arm encircle the body of the pupil as the full twist is completed (Figure 75c and d). After practice the supporter is usually able to release the pupil just after passing the half twist position, and then gradually to release him earlier and earlier.

The hand support can also help the pupil to keep the body in line with the centre of the bed at take-off instead of kicking to the left if the twist is to the left.

Support for Back Pullover

The back pullover, although a simple move for most performers, is a backward rotational move, and it is possible that at the beginning of the learning stage the inexperienced person may, just after take-off, decide that it will not work.

To help overcome this problem Figures 76a–d show a simple support. Figure 76a shows the pupil in the landing position on the bed and the coach standing level with the pupil, one hand close by or touching the pupil's legs and the other hand grasping the raised hand of the pupil. As soon as the pupil has landed the coach gives a little kip, and helps direct the legs of the pupil up and back. As soon as the pupil is clear of the bed, the coach places the hand which pushed on the legs just above the buttocks of the pupil and

Figure **76** Simple support for back pullover

either follows the pupil around or gives a boost to the rotation (Figures 76b and c). The coach's hand grasping the hand of the pupil helps to keep a good height to the move and supports the pupil on the way down to the landing. The coach's hand, which was on the back of the pupil, is then moved to support the shoulders of the pupil to ensure a good landing (Figure 76d).

This type of support does not usually have to be used for very long, but it does prove useful for skills like the back pullover and avoids unpleasant landings with consequent lack of confidence in some pupils.

A further progression could be to take the pupil round to another back drop landing thus completing a somersault backwards from back drop to back drop.

Hands and Knees Drop, Forward Turnover with Support

The main problem with learning the hands and knees drop forward turnover is the elimination of travel. Provided that the performer lands on the hands and knees in the position shown in Figure 77a and holds that position for the take-off there will usually be no problem. There is however a tendency for all learners to land with the seat a little back towards the heels and the shoulders a little further back from the hands than the position shown in the figure. As the legs are extended into the bed the trunk is allowed to ride forward so that the shoulders are ahead of the hands and both the upper thigh and the arm are pushing back into the bed, so that although there is a forward rotation there is also travel. Since the shoulders are well forward the pupil usually drops the head and bends the arms and the travelled rotation is also very low. The experienced performer can stay on the spot without losing height from almost any landing; this is not the case with the beginner.

In order to counteract the above faults the coach can hand stop the move and help the pupil feel the correct take-off and flight. The coach stands level with the performer with one hand in front of the shoulder and one hand just ahead of the hips. Figures 77a and b show the hand positioning, left hand on the shoulder and right hand ahead of the hips. In order to get a take-off the coach can either kip the pupil up and down once or twice or the pupil can drop from standing into the all-fours position for an immediate take-off. In order to counteract the lean the pupil is asked to concentrate on getting the correct landing position (from the same take-off as a front drop). The coach applies a backward pressure against the pupil's shoulder as the take-off is made and helps to guide the pupil upwards with the shoulders whilst helping the

Figure **77** Hands and knees drop forward turnover with support

hips also to rise up into the air higher than the shoulders and thus to get a high on the spot rotation (Figure 77c). Figure 77c1 shows arm position as seen from the front. As the point shown in Figure 77d is reached the supporting hands are changed over so that the coach's right hand is behind the shoulder and the left hand is under the lower back (Figure 77e). The pupil can then be set down on the back, or with more practice, even on to the feet. After some practice the correct take-off will be consolidated and the pupil should be able to perform the move on the spot.

Front Somersault Hand Support

The front somersault should not be attempted without support. After the forward turn-over to back drop and the forward turnover with tuck to seat have been mastered the pupil is ready to try the supported front somersault.

In Figure 78a the supporter's right hand holds the pupil's left hand (as Figure 70) and the supporter's left hand is rested against the pupil's left shoulder. The hand on the shoulder is to encourage the pupil to lift up into the take-off instead of dropping the shoulders. The hand is not meant to resist rotation. The pupil takes off for a lifting roll-ing start, making sure that the rolling action is upwards. After take-off the pupil tucks up and rotates further. Figure 78b shows the supporter reaching up to support the lower back of the pupil and to control the descent to the bed. Figure 78c shows the pupil at a lower point in the descent and the placing of the supporter's hand. From this point on the pupil should open out for the landing, with the supporter still in contact. If the hand on the lower back of the pupil is not sufficient to slow the rate of rotation enough and the pup-il tends to rebound still rotating forwards the supporter can place the left hand under the left arm of the pupil for even more retarda-tion (Figure 78d). It is wise to use two sup-porters for the beginning stages. This not only gives better support: it helps to train supporters. The weaning process can then go from two supporters to one, with the second supporter coming in from the side of the trampoline for the landing. Then the second supporter only comes in from the side if needed. The main supporter releases the hand hold but stays on the bed to give imm-ediate support if the pupil falters. Then the supporter comes in from the side for the landing. The crash mat may be used at this stage so that the landing is cushioned. Only when the coach, as well as the pupil, is satisfied that the whole move is safely learned can all

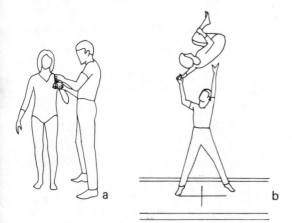
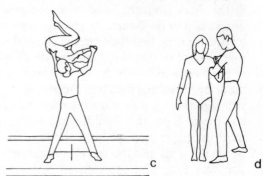

Figure **78** Front somersault hand support

support be relinquished. Go back to support if it is considered necessary for safety.

The rig may also be used as a support for the front somersault. It is perfectly adequate but takes far longer to set up each time. The pupil can also over rotate without the supporter being able to control the extra rotation. The crash mat can be used in conjunction with the rig for extra comfort and safety on landing.

The front somersault can also be supported in the final stages at the waist with a towel or belt around the waist or a firm hold on the shorts or track suit (see Figure 79). This stage can be the final one before the pupil is allowed to go it alone with the coach still standing on the bed or the frame to get in quickly if support is needed for the landing.

The normal safety requirements for finally checking performance before relinquishing total support still apply. Once the coach

sault for the first time the idea of getting the lower body up in the air to bring it level with the upper body. It does help to counteract the idea that a back somersault is performed by dropping or throwing the head back.

However it is best used by an experienced coach since there is a danger that the pupil might throw the head back at the coach and the coach might then drop the pupil as a take-off is made. Figure 80a shows the starting stance and hold. The coach takes a firm grip on the clothing of the pupil at waist level or puts a towel or judo belt around the waist to grip on. The grip is at centre waist. The other arm is then placed in a firm, but not uncomfortable, hold around the neck.

Before starting, explain the technique to the pupil. This will help to avoid excessive throw back of the pupil's head or leaning back at take-off. It is also necessary to explain to the pupil that a jump must be made rather than the feet be lifted off the bed. If the

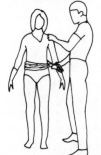

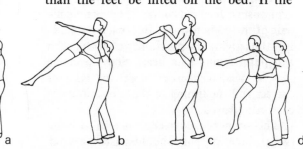

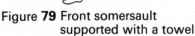

Figure **79** Front somersault
supported with a towel

Figure **80** Starting stance and hold for back
somersault

has left the bed it is not possible for him to get back on in time if the pupil fails. The crash mat can be used at any stage for further support, especially after the coach has left the frame.

Hand Support Behind Neck for Back Somersault Preparation

This support is very good for giving a pupil who is preparing to attempt the back somer-

shoulders and head are thrown back the coach may lose the hold on the neck through excessive pressure being put on the thumb. If the feet are lifted at take-off the pupil may drop downwards and again the coach be forced to let go.

Figure 80b shows the pupil just after take-off. The hips have been displaced forwards and the push of the legs into the bed causes the body to rise up in the air rotating backwards. The coach's right hand on the waist helps to lift the pupil forwards, and the left hand on the shoulder helps to direct the shoulders and head in an upward direction. The right arm of the supporter is kept straight so that the hips do not sag during the take-off, and the left arm is held high to keep the shoulders well up. The stance of the supporter with one leg behind the other is necessary to counteract any strong backward push by the performer and also to enable the supporter to step in under the pupil at maximum height if necessary.

Figure 80c shows the pupil in the tucked position which will accelerate the rotation of the body to ensure completion of the somersault. This acceleration may cause an increase in the pressure of the neck against the hand of the supporter, who must be ready to take the extra strain without letting the pupil feel insecure or dropping the pupil.

Figure 80d shows the supporter bringing the pupil back to a foot landing. It is necessary to ensure that the hips of the pupil are kept pushed forward so that there is no collapse of the body towards the coach on landing, thus giving the possibility of both coach and pupil falling in a heap. Some practice may be needed in order to get the take-off correct and the timing of the tuck and open correctly phased.

This support used in conjunction with the two persons support should ensure a safer preparation for the back somersault.

Back Somersault with Support

On no account should any pupil be allowed to attempt a back somersault without first going through the progressions and then having support. A fall on a back somersault can cause very serious injury and no pupil should be exposed to this risk.

The progressions include the back drop, the flat back drop, the back pullover to stomach and to feet. The coach should then make sure that the pupil understands the

process for initiating backward rotation. This can be done by holding the neck and the waist of the pupil from behind and then getting the pupil to jump the legs forwards so that they rise into the air. Having established that, take the stance as shown in Figure 81a. Supporter's right hand grasps the left hand of the pupil (see Figure 81b). Supporter's left hand is placed on the buttocks of the pupil slightly behind the seam of the leotard or shorts. Figure 81b shows the exact position. The lower hand will then be able to give a boost to the pupil if there is lack of rotational force. It is wise to use two supporters at first rather than one.

The pupil takes off with the legs and hips moving forward so that backward rotation is initiated. The supporter keeps pushing, either gently or hard, if necessary (Figure 81c). As the pupil passes over the top of the rotational circle the supporter moves the left hand to the shoulder of the pupil so that the

Figure **81** Support for back somersault

head is kept high allowing the body to drop past it (Figure 81d). If the hand is kept on the left shoulder of the pupil it can easily slide under the arm as the pupil descends lower (Figure 81e) and provide a very strong support for the landing, helping to stop any over rotation. The skills of the back somersault are also detailed on p. 52.

The rig can be used for the back somersault. In conjunction with the crash mat this provides a very strong support. It does however take some time to set up for each person and is very strenuous for the coach compared with the hand support. It does provide an opportunity for some performers to get the feel of relatively free performance before going ahead to the next stage, free performance.

As with the front somersault, support can be given with a belt round the waist or by gripping the shorts or track suit (see Figure 82). This can be seen as a further progression

Figure **82** Back somersault supported with a towel

towards free performance. As a support method it is preferred by some coaches. Although it is a good method it does not have the control of the hand to hand method.

Crash Dive Support

The crash dive is often performed with a distinct pull down at take-off. In order to help counteract this fault manual support can be used. Figure 83a shows the pupil and the supporter with the normal front somersault support hand grip. For a pull down which is not too strong the use of the hand hold is often sufficient for the pupil to learn to correct the take-off. The supporting presence of the coach can help the pupil to raise the shoulders at take-off rather than drop them. This will enable the pupil to watch the bed longer, to rotate more slowly and to make a more correct landing on the shoulders instead of the lower back. The supporter tries to help ensure that the pupil lifts the arms at take-off instead of just letting them hang down, creating a down motion at the start of the move. The main advantage to the pupil is that he is helped to feel the correct speed of rotation and the direction of the lift, which might not have been possible without the help of the coach and the supporting lift as shown in Figure 77b. Over

Figure **83** Crash dive support

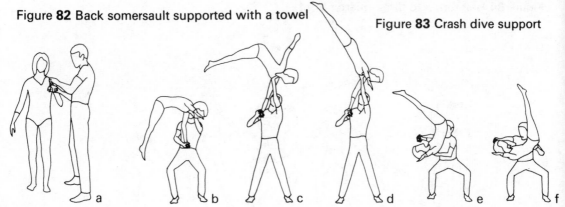

a   b   c   d   e   f

rotation can be further slowed by the placing of the other hand of the coach on the seat of the pupil before the landing is made and exerting an upward pressure (Figure 83c).

In situations where the pupil is dropping the head and shoulders or throwing them down excessively it may be necessary for the coach to place the left hand on the chest of the pupil before take-off so that a stronger retardation of rotation may be made (Figure 83c). This retardation is maintained until the pupil is just about horizontal, when the chest support may be released and the normal speed of rotation continued (Figure 83d). The pupil will usually get to know the speed of rotation and take-off power related to this speed and soon be able to act independently of the coach. Do not relinquish support too soon and use it again if necessary.

Half Turn into Three-Quarter Front Somersault Support

The beginning stance and hand grip (shown in Figure 84a) are the same as for the back somersault with full twist and for the full twist to back drop. For the first few take-offs it is easier for the pupil to turn a little away from the supporter and look behind at the bed as in the first stages of the half twist to front drop. This also ensures that the pupil is looking at the bed from the start of the move rather than having to pick up sight of the bed during the flight.

Figure 84b shows the pupil just after take-off, a small amount of twist completed, rising into the air with the body straight, having pushed well down into the bed without lean back or cast. This is important; for the start to be correct all the above actions must be completed fully. It will ensure that the body can rise into the air easily so that the pupil feels the lift and does not try to kink in order to get over on to the back. Figure 84c shows the body still rising, the supporter having both hands in contact with the pupil. At the top of the rise into the air (Figure 84d) the supporter is just losing contact with the pupil and there is a slight delay before the pupil will begin the descent. This is often the point at which the pupil may suffer from loss of determination to succeed. Figure 84e shows the pupil about to land on the rounded back, with the supporter checking for over rotation.

The half turn into three-quarter front somersault has proved to be one of those apparently simple, but in reality often difficult, moves for some pupils.

This move is an early progression into the back somersault with full twist.

Figure **84** Half turn into three-quarter front somersault support

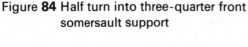

Three-Quarter Back Somersault Support

Although the three-quarter back somersault is considered to be an easy movement, it is quite difficult for many people to learn without some fear of falling on the head, since the rotation is so slow and there is a considerable wait before the bed is sighted.

Figure 85a shows the starting position for the support move. The spotter holds the clothing of the pupil at waist level with the hand further away from the pupil and places the other hand just below the curve of the buttocks, the same support as for later stages of the back somersault support.

Figure 85b shows the pupil just after take-off with the spotter keeping the same hand holds and in a good strong body position. By the stage shown in Figure 85c the hands have to change position; the right hand moves to the higher position on the back and the left hand moves to the lower, as clearly shown in Figure 85d. With the hands in the position shown in Figure 85d and some grasp of the clothing, the rate of rotation of the pupil may be adjusted to make sure that the landing is level. Downward pressure on the shoulders will slow up the rotation, and downward pressure on the buttocks will speed up rotation. It is also possible, for the first few attempts, to bring the pupil down to land in the hands and knees position as shown in Figure 85e. This is very useful for the first stages of learning since the landing is easier on the hands and knees, because slight errors of over or under rotation do not matter as much as on the straight landing. With practice the coach will soon learn just how much adjustment of the rate of rotation is needed.

Barani Support

In addition to giving support to the pupil, hand supporting also helps the pupil to realise in which direction the turn is being made.

Figure 86a shows the hand grip with the supporter's right hand holding the pupil's left hand, with the same hand grip as for the front somersault. This indicates that the direction of turn will be to the pupil's left. Figures 86b–e show the sequence for a straight barani. It can also be performed in the tucked and piked positions. An easy approach can be made via the tucked or piked front somersault with late half twist. The pupil performs a tucked or piked front somersault and as the opening out is made the pupil turns towards the support. For the hand grip shown above the turn will be to the left. The late twist enables the pupil to get a good lifted front somersault with no cast or

Figure **85** Three-quarter back somersault support

Figure **86** Barani support

thought of twisting until the last part of the somersault. It avoids the problem of the pupil turning the head immediately on take-off and losing orientation.

Most pupils who learned the barani from the arab Spring approach are mistaken about the direction of the twist. This seems to be a result of a visual illusion and has led to many problems with the learning of the front somersault with full twist.

Practise the late half twist for a number of times, making sure that the pupil is performing the twist without your aid although you are supporting the somersault. Gradually get the pupil to watch the bed at the start of the twist and on subsequent attempts to keep it in vision for longer and longer until it is sighted throughout the whole move.

Figure 86d shows the spotter reaching up for the pupil to help with the descent and Figure 86e shows help with the landing. Lessening of support can be made by the supporter holding less tightly and, later still, releasing the hand hold after take-off. Let the pupil know when you are at the stage of re-leasing the grip so that he does not try to reach for your hand in panic in mid-flight. This support is the starting support for the front somersault with full twist.

Front Somersault with Full Twist Support (Hand)

The hand spotted front somersault with full twist is a progression from the barani with hand support. Figure 87a shows the standard hand hold and starting position for the front somersault or barani with hand support. Figure 87b shows the barani supported and the pupil just about to start the twist. Figures 87c and d show the pupil completing the half twist. At this point the pupil has to carry on to twist in the same direction as he is already rotating. For the first few attempts there may be a problem for some pupils due to confusion about the direction of the barani twist. This may be corrected by letting the pupil land in the half twist, barani position (Figure 87d) and then perform a jump with a half twist in the same direction. This will help to consolidate the correct direction of twist for the pupil without having to work it out in mid-air. Repeat the barani support and let the pupil try to make the extra twist just before landing. Keep working at this until the pupil is confident enough to let the twist flow all the way round (Figures 87d–f). The hand hold as the twist progresses lifts the arm of the pupil so that, on landing, the held

Figure **87** Hand support for front somersault with full twist

hand of the pupil is raised and in the normal position of a front somersault landing, with the hands twisted further round than usual. At first the supporter may find that there is a tendency for the supported arm to be wrapped round the upper chest of the pupil. This can be eliminated with a little practice. As with all supported moves the idea is to eliminate the support gradually so that the pupil can perform alone.

Figure **88** Hand support for back somersault with full twist

Back Somersault with Full Twist Support (Hand)

Before attempting this support the pupil should be well able to perform a back somersault straight, a barani and a front somersault with half twist. Support shown turning to the left. A number of progressions are also necessary before the whole move with support is attempted as shown in Figures 88b–g. To adopt the hand grip shown in Figure 88a, start with the coach taking the hand grip for the front somersault, his right hand holding the left hand of the pupil. The pupil then

turns 180° to the right to face in the opposite direction. The pupil can now turn 360° to the left to end up facing in the same direction as shown but with the hand held by the coach across the front of the body.

Work through the following progressions until they can be performed easily with the height shown in the figures. It is important that the height shown in the figures is attained to ensure adequate lift to allow a flowing movement to be performed.

[1] From the position shown in Figure 88a jump with a half twist followed by a tucked front somersault.

[2] From position Figure 88a jump with a half twist followed by a barani (tucked or open).

[3] From position Figure 88a turn the upper body round in the direction of twist and perform a half twist into a front somersault.

[4] Perform the half twist into a front somersault, starting the twist at take-off.

[5] As 3 (Figure 88a) for the start but perform a barani.

[6] Perform the half twist into the barani, starting the twist at take-off, following the sequence shown in Figures b–g.

Figures 88b and c show the half twist being performed at take-off and Figures 88d–g show the barani as in the barani support (Figures 86b–e). Some pupils will need all the progressions and some will need only some of them. Practice will help to ensure that the pupil can perform the whole move smoothly as shown in the sequence a–g. The whole move can be learned in the rig as an alternative.

The half twist into crash dive is a good practice for the start of the back somersault with full twist, also the back somersault straight. The emphasis is on straight without any arching of the back.

Back Somersault with Full Twist in Safety Harness

The back somersault with full twist may be taught in the safety harness as well as with manual support. The basic requirements for performance are the same as for the manual support method. The pupil must be able to perform a half turn into duck under with an early sighting of the bed. A barani is also a requirement turning the same way as the half turn into duck under. The first series of Figures 89a–f show the pupil working in the safety harness to perform the half turn into duck under or front somersault.

During take-off the pupil turns the head and shoulders to the left as shown in the figures (or right if that is the way the pupil normally twists). The twist must be sufficiently strong to cause the body to complete a half twist by the time the body has reached the amount of rotation shown in Figure 89f. The body passes through the position shown in Figures 89c–e, with the bed in sight. The turn is completed as in Figure 89f. The pupil is still looking at the bed and can either duck under for a back landing or tuck up for a front somersault finish. It is best after a few successful half turns into duck under to move ahead to half turn into front somersault so that the amount of rotation necessary is approximated. The coach has to make sure that the ropes of the safety harness are kept just taut enough for the pupil to feel supported, neither slack nor too tight so that the pupil cannot sink into the bed or rebound. Remember, if the pupil is going to land on the back an additional amount of rope must pass through the hands so that the landing

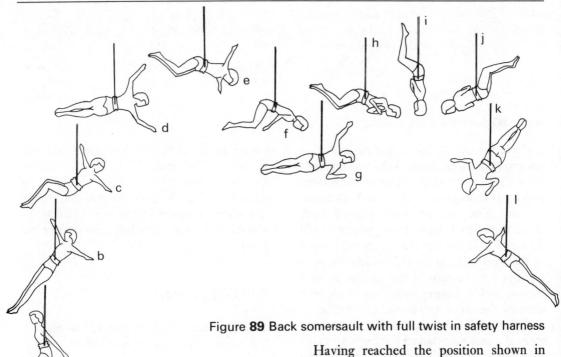

Figure **89** Back somersault with full twist in safety harness

may be made easily. Once the half turn into front somersault has been mastered it is necessary to move ahead into the next stage (Figures 89g–l). A slightly more powerful somersault is needed so that the second half of the move may be accomplished easily, the pucked or straight position, needing a little more rotational power than the tucked position at the end of the first stage.

Refer to Figure 89d and it can be seen that Figure 89g would follow on in the pattern of movement, provided that the more powerful rotation was initiated and a slightly more powerful turn of the shoulders was made at take-off. It must be emphasised that the total effort for the twist is quite small since the radius about which the body twists is quite small by comparison with the somersault radius.

Having reached the position shown in Figure 89g with arms wide and somersault rotating well enough, it only remains to pull in the wide arms close to the chest for the twist to speed up and enable the full twist to be completed (Figures 89h–k). In Figure 89l the performer is about to land on the bed.

As the performer becomes more accomplished the body can be kept straight throughout the whole move as shown in Figures 112a–n.

Back Kaboom Support

The back kaboom, although a simple move, can be very tricky for some pupils. It is one of those skills which seem to elude some and yet are easy for others.

To make the learning stage easier it is good sense to give support in the initial stages. The first support is to ensure that the leg kick is giving enough rotation to complete the rotation to feet. It is only three-quarters of a somersault but the first rotation can be on to

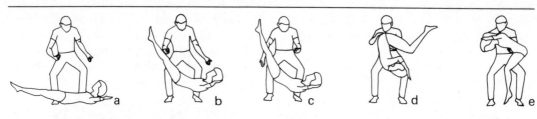

Figure **90** Back Kaboom support

the head instead of clear of the head. Figure 90a shows the kick down to the bed on landing with the pupil's legs rising up to be stopped by the forearm of the coach at about 45°–60°. The legs are then pushed back down to the bed. Repeat this process until the rotation of the legs is very strong judged by the amount of force with which the pupil's legs hit the arm of the coach. Instant tension and a sharper kick down will help increase the speed and power of rotation.

Figure 90d shows the placing of the arms when the coach has asked the pupil to make an attempt for the complete move. The coach's left arm will contact the pupil's waist and the right arm will help push the pupil over to his feet. Often the pupil will grasp the left arm of the coach. This does not matter and will stop when more confidence is gained. The final support is shown in Figure 90e when the coach's right arm supports the shoulder of the pupil to help gain the upright position.

Ball Out Support

Many attempts have been made to support the ball out but it has proven difficult. However the experienced coach can make sure of the support shown in Figures 91a–d and e–k.

First it is necessary to get the performer to

Figure **91** Ball out support

perform a back drop with high supported rise to feet. It is important that the performer is able to produce enough kick to enable him to rise until his waist is at the height of the coach's shoulder, with the body straight. This will ensure that there is enough height and rotational force to enable the pupil, when tucking at the right point in flight, to complete the one and a quarter somersault. The coach must be able to 'kip' in the body position shown in Figures 91a and 91e. The pupil must land with the arm, supported by the coach, held straight and not pulled down into the chest. If the arm is pulled down it will pull the coach down and make the support difficult.

Having mastered the high rise from back drop, move on to the next phase (Figures 91e–k). The first two figures show the pupil and coach in the same position as before. The pupil has however kicked harder and is ready to tuck up in order to speed up the rotation. Figures 91g and h show the pupil beginning to tuck up and also show the height reached. The height is necessary for the easy support by the coach as well as the easy performance of the ball out. If there is too little height the coach will find support very strenuous and

the pupil will find that there is a tendency for the rotation to be a little short. Figures 91i–k indicate that the supporting techniques are very similar to that of the tucked front somersault with support.

Preparation for the Cody with Hand Support: One or Two Persons

The cody is a skill of such complexity that many find it somewhat frightening. It is therefore most sensible to approach its performance carefully. Figures 92a–e show a simple approach for a coach with a small person. For larger pupils it is best to use two supporters.

In Figure 92a the pupil has just dropped into a seat drop position and is about to be kipped up by the coach. In Figure 92b the pupil has been caught by the coach and is being held tightly whilst the bed is further depressed to assist the effort of turning the pupil over. Figures 92c–e show the coach using the rebound of the bed to lift the pupil and to make the turning over of the pupil much easier. It is important to make sure that the grip on the pupil is moved from the

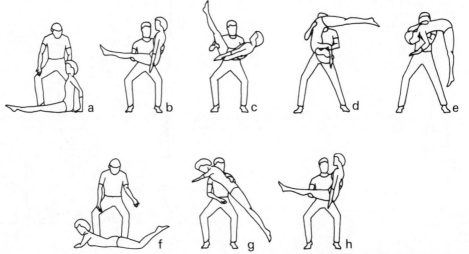

Figure **92** Hand support for the cody

lower back and upper thigh to the shoulder and lower back, as shown in Figure 92d. It is important to ensure that the pupil's head is kept high and well away from the bed as the turnover is made.

Figures 92f–h show the next stage where the pupil is caught on rising from the front drop landing. From the coach's point of view good kipping skills are necessary so that the pupil is not hit hard by too early a kip and neither is the rebound killed by too late a kip. The pupil will also need to be able to use the leg kick down when in the position shown in Figure 92f to ensure that rotation is good. One of the most important points is to make sure that the pupil rebounds high enough to make the catch easy. A low rebound will cause the spotter to have to bend down and try to catch the pupil. In all the above figures it is possible to use two spotters. The second one stands opposite the first. The kipping

skills of both must be good. Unco-ordinated kipping kills the rebound or causes a rebound with cast.

One and Three-Quarter Front Somersault in the Rig

This skill is the prerequisite for the barani out and the rudolf out fliffes. It is also necessary for many mid-difficult routines to provide the way into skills such as the ball out barani, the double ball out, the ball out barani out. It is necessary to use the belt in the teaching of this skill to ensure the safety of the pupil. Preparatory moves are the tucked front somersault and the tucked one and a quarter front somersault. It is important that those moves are well lifted and phased to give an acceleration in the middle and a deceleration for the landing. Especially on the one

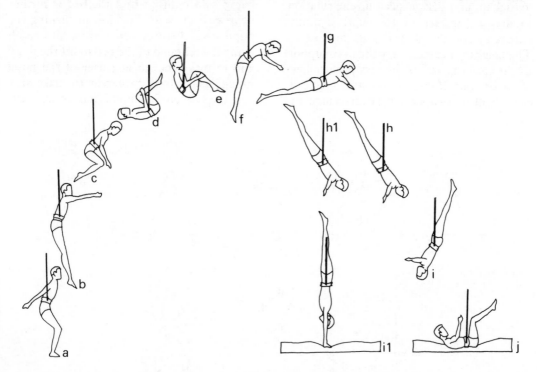

Figure **93** One and three-quarter front somersault in the rig

and a quarter front somersault it is important that the pupil drops down on the crash mat with good clearance rather than lands just as soon as the body opens out from the tucked position.

Figures 93a and b show a standard take-off with a good open-bodied rise into the air without any hurry to tuck or any sign of pulling down. This will help to ensure that there is plenty of angular momentum and thus plenty of potential for acceleration. Figures 93c–e show the tucking of the body to speed up the rotation so that the performer is coming round to the vertical position still tucked, and at the top of the rise. This means that there is now too much rotation for the one and a quarter landing, and leads to the necessity for the coach to pull on the rope to slow the descent in case it is under rotated or over rotated. Until the pupil has had a certain amount of experience there is a tendency for the speed of rotation to vary. This could cause damage to the back on landing. In any case the coach needs to take precautions erring on the side of safety rather than chance.

As the pupil opens out from the tucked position (Figures 93f–h), and the coach pulls on the rope to give a controlled descent, the pupil is able to stretch the body whilst keeping the crash mat in sight as the descent is made. A folding of the body at the waist will allow for the landing on the crash mat with the body in the pucked position (Figure 90j).

An intermediate stage is shown in Figures 93h1, i1). The pupil is asked to come out to a handstand position with a very strong support from the coach so that the idea of looking at the bed, as the body is straightened from the tucked position, may be consolidated. After contact is made in the handstand position the coach releases the support and the performer drops gently down for the same landing as in Figure 93j. When the pupil is well aware of the look out and landing, less support is given: the pupil reaches out but does not put the hands down, and then ducks for the landing. Gradually the support is lessened until the landing is made regularly and safely by the pupil. Only then after the whole move has been performed many times with the rope slack but the coach ready to give assistance may the move be attempted into the crash mat which is pushed in under the pupil for the landing. Once again the weaning process is used to ensure that confidence is gained and any slight inaccuracy of landing is cushioned. When both pupil and coach are satisfied, the whole move may be attempted without any support. Go back to support in the rig, or with the crash mat, if there are any problems.

5

Skills to and from the Back and Stomach with and without Twists

Three-Quarter Back Somersault (0.3)

The three-quarter back somersault is a difficult move to perform high and under perfect control. It is a simple move and its simplicity demands precision. The landing must be accurate or it will be accompanied by pain. The move must not be under or over rotated. There is no margin for error as there is on the landing of the move, which is its equivalent in forward rotation, the three-quarter front somersault or crash dive. A

slight under rotation is less of a problem than a slightly over rotated landing position.

The figures show the sequence of arm actions and body positions in flight. Take-off is normal but the amount of rotation is very slight. Figures 94b and c show the lift of the arms soon after take-off, just before they are placed in line with the body during the middle of the flight, to give a good line. Note that the head is not thrown back at take-off but is kept in line or even very slightly forward. This helps to keep the body in a straight line

Figure **94** Three-quarter back somersault

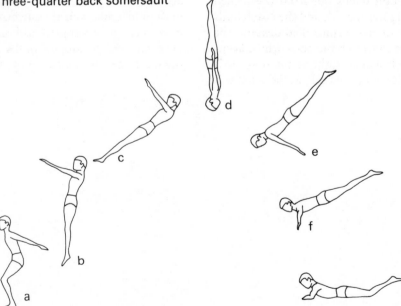

from head to toe. The amount of hip displacement at take-off is very small but the leg drive is fairly strong to lift the whole body in a straight position up and through the required rotation, without any need for arching or kinking, until the legs are bent just before the landing (to provide the eccentric kick down for rotation to feet or further) (Figure 94g).

Figure 94d shows the body vertically upside down. The head is tipped very slightly back to give sight of the bed. The body should be at the apex of the jump and about to descend with increasing acceleration towards the landing. It is often at this point that the performer recognises over or under rotation and can kink to increase speed or stretch the arms to decrease speed of rotation for a comfortable landing.

Figures 94e–g show the arms being lifted away from the body for the landing in which they support the head and can be used to push against the bed for rotation to feet or further. The main rotational force is provided by the leg kick, not the arm push. Keep the body taut right into the landing to ensure a good rebound and efficient transfer of the leg kick as in the front drop to feet. Any loss of tautness leads to *absorption* of rebound force and eccentric force with consequent loss of efficiency.

Backward Rotation from the Front Landing Position (Cody Kick)

The same principle for generation of rotational force is used from the front landing position as for the back landing position, the transfer of momentum from the legs to the whole body. Figure 95 shows the body in the front landing position ready to beat the legs down hard to generate backward rotation. The dotted lines show the extent of the leg movement. As in the back landing the body must be held taut for the landing and then

further action taken to kick the lower legs towards the bed, stopping them just before they reach the bed. If the body is taut, the upper part of the body will start to rise faster than the lower part generating backward rotation.

Figure **95** Backward rotation from the front landing position

If the seat is allowed to rise up into the air because the gluteal muscles have not been sufficiently contracted then the rotation will be reduced. It is not possible to gain extra height by the use of the legs, and on the front drop landing it is necessary to see that the technique is used correctly to avoid loss of height and rotation.

Obviously some rotational force is generated by use of the arms to push into the bed but the main force is produced by the leg action. Up to triple somersaults and some multiple twisting fliffes have been performed from the front landing by the more able performers. In top level competition there is less use made of somersaults from the front landing than from the back landing.

Cody (0.5)

The cody is a back somersault from the stomach to the feet. It was named because the first person to carry it out was an American called Dale Cote, or so the story goes. Effectively it is a one and a quarter back somersault with the extra quarter of a somersault at the beginning of the move. It is the extra quarter at the start which makes the move difficult for beginners. Body tension on landing is most important as in the ball out. The power for the rotation is produced by the lower leg being suspended above the bed of the trampoline for the landing thus automatically giving a downwards eccentric force as the impact is made. The power is further increased by a sharp downward kick on impact if needed. The landing position is illustrated in Figure 96a.

Back drop to feet with body straight and back drop to front drop with straight body are very important skills to have acquired before starting on the learning of the cody. The arms play very little part in the initiation of rotation, although to the uninitiated this may not seem to be the case. It has been suggested that the kaboom technique is used after the three-quarter back somersault landing. There is no real evidence that this does happen. It is more likely to be the rocking bed as the kick is made. The legs are usually lifted to make the kick and the reaction from this will, of course, cause a reaction in the bed. Study of ultra-slow motion film has so far produced conflicting opinions of the same actions. It is also mechanically obvious that it is very difficult to get an efficient push with the arms since the upper body is departing from the trampoline bed first, if there is good tension, making a powerful push against a departing surface mechanically unlikely.

From the position shown in Figure 96a, the legs are held tense or kicked sharply down to initiate backward rotation so that the body rises straight into the air (Figure 96b). As soon as this has taken place the body is tucked tightly so that a fast rotation will occur (Figures 96c and d). It must be stressed that for real effectiveness the straight position must be held until at least about 70° of rotation has taken place. When the tuck is then pulled the rotation is sharp enough to carry the pupil easily over the usual sticking point, which is just before the vertically upside-down position is reached (Figure 96d). Figures 96e and f show the early come out from the tuck which is particularly attractive on the cody to make the landing in Figure 96g.

The beginner will often be anxious to get into the tucked position and will fail to achieve a good start. This will mean that even with a tight tuck the rotation is only slow and the pupil must hold on to the tuck to get round. This problem should be cured in the supported stage of the learning process (*see* p. 79).

The cody was at one time a very popular move in voluntary routines and many variations were seen including triple twisting, half in half out, and triple somersaults. It has however lost favour, being superseded by the foot to foot fliffes to gain slightly more tariff.

Figure **96** The cody

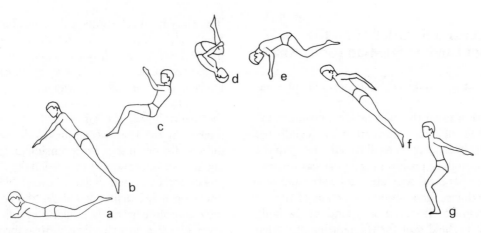

Crash Dive, Three-Quarter Front Somersault Straight (0.3)

The crash dive or three-quarter front somersault straight is one of the most elegant moves in trampolining when done well. It is a simple move and so, often, it is not performed well.

The basic work for the crash dive is the front drop straight, performed without any break in the body line from just after take-off until the landing. The main problem in the performance of the crash dive is that it tends to be pulled down into the bed whatever the height of the jump and consequently tends to be slightly overturned on landing.

From the take-off position shown in Figure 97a, the arms are swung well up and forward with head up and hips slightly displaced backwards. This action will give a position immediately after take-off as shown in Figure 97b. Alternatively the arms may be left high for the landing immediately before take-off. This affords a good body line but is more difficult to control, and can lead to some pull down with consequent loss of easy height.

For the best line of the body it is important not to try to lift the heels at take-off but to endeavour to keep the head in line with the body and to get a feeling of an almost vertical body as the lift takes place. The straight body should rise into the air and 'hang' momentarily at the top (Figures 97c and d). The position is held as the body starts to descend, until an almost vertical position is reached (Figure 97e). As the body passes through the vertical, piking is started (Figure 97f), and increased for further rotation (Figure 97g), and the landing is made (Figure 97h). Just before the landing the legs are bent to put the body in a ready position for the next take-off.

Figure **97** Crash dive, three-quarter front somersault straight

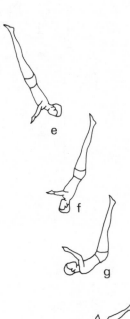

Alternatively the legs may be kept straight (*see* ball out take-off techniques).

Much work will be needed to perfect the crash dive. It is very easy to lean a little at take-off and to duck the head early. It may be necessary to give support to those learning it to avoid the two faults mentioned above. It is usually very necessary to give support to the person who has already learned the move and has the faults set. Support helps the performer to feel the correct take-off 'hang' and duck under. The methods are described under crash dive support.

Half Twist into Three-Quarter Crash Dive Front Somersault (0.4)

Many performers find this straightforward move a little difficult. However if early sight-ing of the bed is attained and a slow twist is initiated there should be no difficulty.

As the pupil takes off visual contact is kept by looking down at the bed. The arms are swung up and outwards as the shoulders are turned. Enough somersault power is developed to allow the legs to swing up, ahead of the body, whilst the head is turned to keep the initial visual contact (Figures 98a–d). The arms are held wide to keep the twist slow and the body is held straight so that the rotation of the somersault is slow. In this way good vision is retained throughout the move (Figures 98e–h).

As the body descends towards the bed the head is dropped and the back slightly rounded to speed the rotation a little, enabling the pupil to land quite high on the shoulders (Figure 98i). The legs are bent just before the landing is made and the body is held taut for

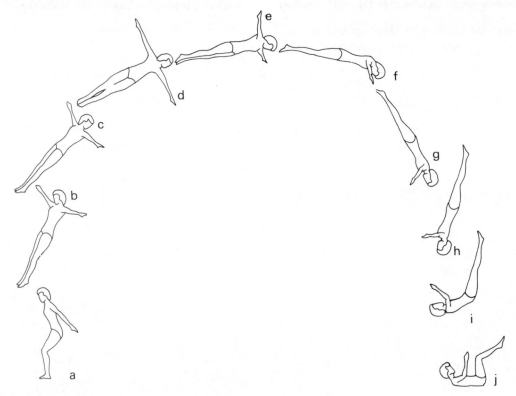

Figure **98** Half twist into three-quarter crash dive front somersault

the best rebound. The bent legs (Figure 98j) are straightened in an upwards direction to increase the height of the rebound and to avoid travel in a forward direction.

This move is a useful one for learning the back somersault with full twist and the one and a half twist into three-quarter front somersault. For learning the back somersault with full twist the forward lifting take-off, with early twist and sight of the bed, is a very good practice and can be lifted even higher and slightly faster in preparation for the whole somersault. The main use is that it helps to avoid a rushed start for the twisting and gives practice in early visual contact.

Forward Rotation from the Back Landing Position (Ball Out Kick)

All forward rotation from the back landing position from back drop to ball out fliffus is generated in the same way but with varying amounts of rotational force. The back drop landing may be made with the legs bent as shown in Figure 99a or with straight legs. The bent leg landing position is the most useful all round since it gives the opportunity to generate more height easily than does the straight leg landing position.

A landing in the bent legs position has two advantages. The bent legs, although still able to generate rotation, are easier to hold in position when the landing is made and the legs can be kicked upwards at the start of the rotation generating technique to give more height than is possible from a rebound only. With the straight leg landing position shown in dotted lines, it is possible to generate plenty of rotational power but less easy to gain height unless the performer is very flexible and very strong. Flexibility is needed to get the legs, on landing, nearer to the head than is shown in the first dotted line position. Strength is needed to prevent the legs from collapsing towards the body on impact and

also to move them immediately powerfully forwards and upwards whilst still keeping them straight. It is up to each performer and coach to decide which technique seems to him to have the most advantage. If the sharp eyes of the form judges need not be taken into account, the bent leg technique would seem to have all the advantages, especially as the number of rotations needs to be increased. Whatever technique is used a strong mid-section is needed to hold a good position on landing and to provide a well-stabilised base for the kick.

From the position shown in Figure 99 kick the lower leg powerfully upward, immediately extending the legs into the straight position shown by the dotted lines and moving them upwards and forwards away from the trunk. The amount of force needed will depend upon the amount of rotation

Figure **99** Forward rotation from the
back landing position

desired. For rotation with a straight body the legs and trunk should be held straight and tight throughout the flight. This is important for moves like the straight ball out barani or the rudi ball out. For moves with multiple rotations the body should be tucked after leaving the bed so that maximum force is generated. Tucking too early will give acceleration before maximum force for rotation has been gained. The arms can be swung forward and upward in the same direction as the legs, if so desired, possibly giving a useful increase in power if moved whilst in contact with the bed.

A strong static contraction of the trunk muscles will assist transfer of momentum from the legs to the trunk. Allowing the body to arch will lessen the transfer of angular momentum. Make sure that contraction of the trunk muscles occurs before making contact with the bed to gain maximum depression before any rotational force is initiated by the use of the legs.

Forward Turnover from Back to Back (Porpoise) (0.4)

This move is very useful for learning the ball out to feet and the ball out barani. It gives an opportunity to get used to watching the bed whilst turning over in a forward somersault and learning to measure the slight duck of the head for the back landing. This technique is to be used in all front three-quarter moves where the landing is on the back and is critical for safety and for the good performance of the next take-off from the back. It helps to overcome the problem that many beginners have when using the front somersault to back landing, that of overturning the somersault.

From the bent legged, back landing shown in Figure 100a a sharp kick into the air is given to ensure some height for the move. The legs are held firmly and a little out from the lower end of the back; rotation will have already been set up. As the body rises into the air (Figures 100b–d), the vision is kept

forward so that the bed is in sight as much as possible, the head being held slightly forward. By the time the body has reached the point shown in Figure 100e the head is beginning to tilt back a little to keep the bed in sight as the somersault progresses. This is the critical point in measuring the landing. The position shown in Figure 100e illustrates the pupil looking at the bed as the descent is made. A slight ducking of the head to bring it just about in line with the body just precedes the landing which is made with bent legs ready for the next take-off on the spot. This move can be repeated in swing-time and gives good practice in spotting, gaining or travelling skills from the back. It can be used also for practice in developing a leg kick which will help the pupil to gain height when working forwards from the back. It is possible to perform this move with straight legs. It requires a greater trunk flexibility to drop the straight legs back over the head in order to gain height.

Ball Out, Tucked from Forward Turnover or Crash Dive (0.5)

It is easier to perform the ball out from the forward turnover or crash dive than from the back drop. The main reason for this is that the body is already in motion in the same

Figure **100** The porpoise (forward turnover from back to back)

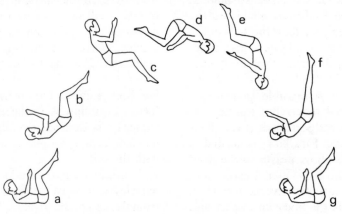

Figure **101** Ball out tucked from forward turnover

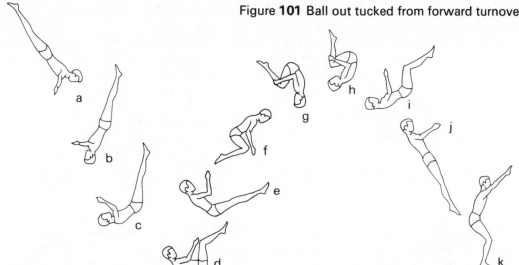

direction as the move following it and the landing followed by the leg kick adds to the momentum already present rather than having to arrest motion in one direction and recommence it in the opposite direction.

The last phase of the turnover or crash dive is shown in Figures 101a–c, indicating watching the bed in Figures 101a–b so that the descent is not blind. Figure 101c shows the head being ducked under when the body is vertical and only just before landing is made (Figure 101d). This technique helps to ensure that the move is not overturned and the body lands shoulders first giving a rolling action into the bed. It also helps to ensure that the performer is able to kick the next part of the move up into the air, rather than being forced into a low travelling move because the legs are forced into a low downwards kick due to the sudden arresting of rotation for a short time as the lower back comes into a heavy contact with the bed. Figure 101d shows the body in position on the back ready to make the kick from the bent legs for the ball out. It can be performed with straight legs but it needs much greater hamstring length to obtain the same direction of leg kick in order to gain height. Figure 101e

shows the body in flight rotating forwards and beginning to pike slightly before tucking (Figures 101f–h) to increase the speed of rotation. The body opens out from the tucked position quite early to decelerate the rotation and to help regain vision of the bed as early as possible. The ball out does tend to be difficult to perform at first due to the back take-off and the body being in the line of vision.

Ball Out Barani (0.6)

The ball out barani is a move that to a large extent depends for its success on the quality of the previous landing. This landing may be from a crash dive or an ordinary back drop. If the landing is from a crash dive make sure that the landing is not overturned at all. This will lead to a lower, travelling performance. The back drop to feet, the back drop forward turnover to back and the simple ball out are all allied and necessary skills to be performed well to assist the good performance of the ball out barani. If the landing is from a back drop make sure that the back drop has not travelled since this again will lead to a

Figure **102** Ball out barani

forward rebound and possible loss of height.

From the landing position shown in Figure 102a a powerful upward and slightly forward kick is made to set up forward somersault rotation. The leg position as shown will normally give a rotational force on landing and the upward kick will give height, as shown in Figure 102b. Figures 102c and d show the tuck, which is for only a short period of time to increase speed of rotation, and then the body starts to open out into the pucked position ready to initiate the twist (Figures 102e and f). As the body extends from the pucked position to the straight position the shoulders are turned in the desired direction of twist and the arms are brought into the sides (Figures 102f–h). The half twist is then easily completed and the straight body is piked a little if necessary to increase the speed of somersault rotation for the landing (Figures 102i–k).

This move needs power and accurate directional kick to be able to carry it out without travel as well as a well-carried out landing. It leads to the ball out barani straight, which again needs considerably more power for success.

Baby Fliffus, Cradle Back (0.6)

The baby fliffus is a movement which is not as common as it used to be in the earlier days of trampolining. It has largely been replaced by the ball out barani. However it is often seen on the Continent and, sometimes, even confused with the ball out barani.

Possibly the cradle back is the best term to use since, in essence, the move consists of a very powerful cradle, with extra height and a tucked pulled to increase the rotation, into a back somersault at the end of the move.

Figure **103** Baby fliffus, cradle back

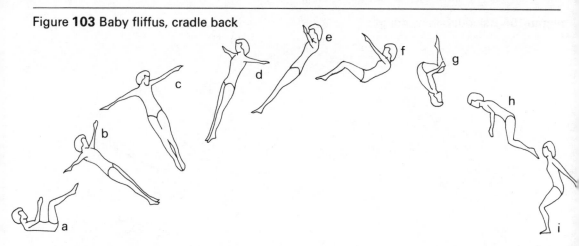

From the back drop or crash dive landing in Figure 103 the legs are kicked up and away powerfully, to set up enough rotation to enable the performer to complete a one and three-quarter somersault. This entails achieving a good extension of the body as it leaves the bed, in order to ensure maximum attainment of height and eccentric force to initiate rotation for the somersault. An early twist is necessary, and this is started whilst the upper body is still in contact with the bed. Initiating the twist is by means of lifting the left shoulder at the same time as the kick is made in Figure 103a. It is important to make sure that the kick is directly in line with the centre line of the bed so that there is no cast in the direction of the leg kick, which may cause the body to move to the right of the centre line in flight.

Figure 103c shows the body just after take-off. There is about a one-quarter twist present which continues with the somersault rotation through Figures 103d and e, until the body is almost horizontal, when the tuck can be started (Figure 103f). Having reached the horizontal position with the body almost straight, the small amount of tuck, shown in Figure 103g, will easily rotate the body quickly, ready for opening out (Figure 103h) with about 85 per cent somersault completed. The landing position (Figure 103i) shows the arms and body ready for the next movement.

Provided that the kick is powerful and the body is kept in the open position, at the start of the flight, acceleration by tucking makes the baby fliffus a fairly easy movement and an attractive one. It permits variety in a routine and the use of two one and three-quarter front somersaults or crash dives.

Practise high early twisting cradles in an open flight position. Keep sight of the bed (head position shown in Figures 103d and e). Similar support to that used for the cody may then be used; that is two supporters to catch and turn the pupil carefully to his feet. The speed of rotation tends to be faster than that of the cody. The tendency to cast is a problem and attention is necessary to avoid an angled kick diagonally to one corner in anticipation of the twist. Get the twist straight and early.

Ball Out Barani Straight (0.7)

Once the ball out barani tucked has been mastered, work should begin on the ball out barani straight. This move needs a lot more power than the other ball out baranis. A very

Figure **104** Ball out barani straight

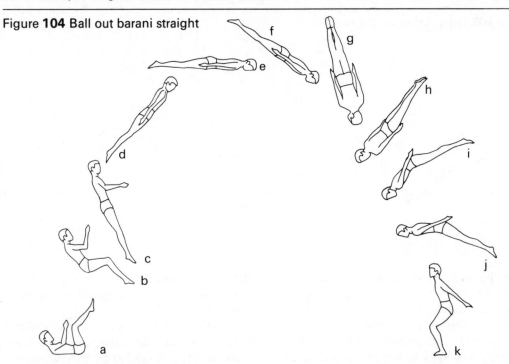

powerful kick from the back is required and then a very early straighten out of the body so that the rest of the move can be carried out with a totally straight body.

From the landing position in Figure 104a a powerful upward kick is made, combined with enough overhang of the legs to ensure that rotation as well as height is obtained. Figure 104b shows the body immediately after take-off with the legs not yet straight. Figure 104c shows the legs completely straight and the body held taut to ensure that all possible transfer of angular momentum is carried out. From that point onwards, Figures 104d–h show the flight with straight body which is relatively easy to hold, provided that a good strong start has been made. Figures 104i–k show the body piking slightly for take off and the landing. The landing will enable the performer to take-off again for the next skill. It is difficult for the learner to get enough somersault rotation to hold the body straight from the start. If the

legs are not aimed high the move tends to be low and the performer has the feeling that the legs are going to touch the bed. There is a tendency to let them bend a little. This same tendency to bend the legs can occur at the position shown in Figure 104f if the performer feels that the rotation is a little slow. Any bending during flight spoils the look and the feel of the move. Sometimes there is travel caused by the anxiety of the performer to get the powerful rotation started at the expense of height by using a slightly forward kick of the legs. Try to avoid this mistake.

Front One and a Quarter Somersault from Back with One and a Half Twists (Rudi Ball Out) (0.8)

For the rudi ball out it is better to be proficient at both the ball out barani straight and the ball out barani in the pucked position. It

Figure **105** Rudi ball out

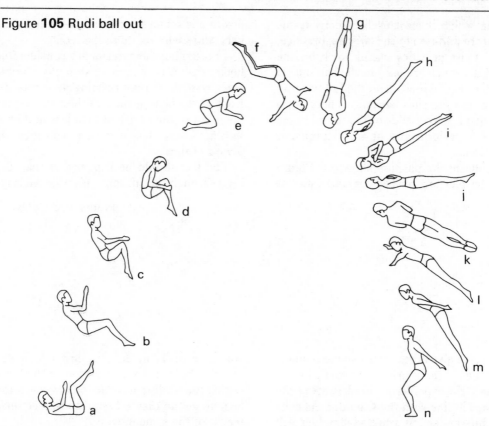

is also necessary to be able to perform the one and a half twisting front somersault.

Figures 105a–d show the powerful take-off with extra upwards kick to give a good height and a tuck to give some early rotation. This is needed to leave plenty of room for the one and a half twists in the straight position and to enable the twists to be initiated from the pucked position by using relative moments of inertia (RMI) twisting techniques.

Practise first the tucked start, with an early kick out to a straight and tight position of the body in the air and just a half twist. Some performers may find that it helps to let the body roll round in an extra half twist making a full twist in all, rather than trying the one and a half twists altogether.

Figures 105e and f show the opening out from the tuck and the beginning of the twist with the shoulders just turning to the left, the arms wide, and the body straightening out. As soon as the arms wrap in and the body straightens, the twist will speed up and the experienced performer should be able to perform the one and a half twists easily. As many advanced moves are combinations of the previously learned moves the learning process is often very quick. Figures 105g–k show the accelerated twist, and 105k–m the opening of the arms and slight piking of the body to slow up the twist and the landing, before take-off for the next skill.

Cat Twist (0.2)

Twisting techniques may be practised from many positions. The back provides an area of twisting which is most useful to any trampolinist. In addition to the twisting practice, the cat twist provides useful work on the same skills which are used in the ball out. It may prove useful in work on the full twisting ball out and the rudi ball out. There is no doubt that any skill adds to the useful range of skilled performance of any competent trampolinist.

Starting in the position shown in Figure 106a, the feet are pushed up and away at

position is achieved or any take-off from the back will easily rotate to the feet.

Throughout the movement a considerable body tension is needed to stop any wobble with consequent poor twisting performance. Look at the bed for most of the twist so that the mind is more relaxed than it would be if sighting were lost for any considerable period of time.

The feet should be kept higher than the head throughout this move if stable landings

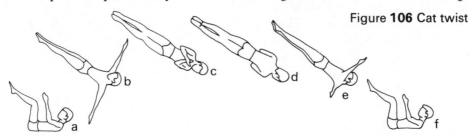

Figure **106** Cat twist

about 45° to give height and a stable bounce. As the body is about to leave contact with the bed the right shoulder is lifted keeping the right arm in line with the shoulder. As contact is broken the left arm and shoulder will move backwards. In order to get the maximum twisting potential the body should be as shown in Figure 106b. Make sure the arms are kept in the crucifix position as the body rises. The head is turned facing the bed to retain visual orientation. Figures 106c and d show the arms being pulled in close to the body to increase the speed of twist. Note that the body is still in a straight line from head to toe. By the time approximately three-quarters of a twist is made, the arms are extended to slow up the speed of twist by increasing the moment of inertia about the longitudinal axis. The last part of the twist is made with the arms out wide to give an easy landing without too much momentum having to be absorbed on contact with the bed.

Figure 106f shows the landing position with the legs in a balanced position ready for the next take-off. It is important that this

are to be easily made. Any lower kick will cause a slight forwards rotation of the body so that the landing is made too low down the back to get an easy rebound to the feet or a repeat of the same move.

The wide arm position and phased twist is a necessary preliminary for the double cat twist. This move is good fun!

Front Kaboom (0.3)

Kabooms are fun skills which add to the repertoire of the pupil. The name is onomatopaoeic, deriving from the sound made by the two contacts of the body on the bed, first the back or chest and then the legs. Kabooms rely on an initial landing followed by a sharp second contact to cause the body to carry on rotating in the same direction as it was before landing. The technique relies on the immediate tensioning of the mid-section of the body as soon as the kick is made. Thus no rotational power is lost.

For the front kaboom practise low, slightly

Figure **107** Front kaboom

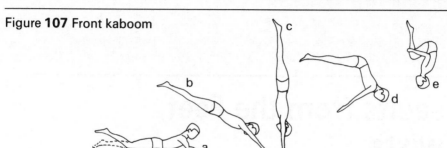

gained front drops, landing with the lower legs slightly raised from the bed. A gentle kick down at this stage will set up a rotational force which can be easily controlled by pushing the hands down into the bed (Figure 107a). Use the same drop down as before but increase the power of the down kick to increase the rotation so that the body begins to rise up into the air towards the handstand position (Figures 107b and c). By the time the pupil has enough power of rotation to rise easily to the handstand with a straight body, the complete kaboom to back is easily possible. Proceed as before through the stages shown in Figures 107a and b but, instead of placing the hands on the bed, let the body tuck or fold so that the speed of rotation is increased (Figures 107d and e) and it is possible to rotate to back, seat or even feet. Remember not to let the pupil anticipate the acceleration too much causing loss of rotational transfer. The very experienced performer can achieve one and three-quarter somersaults, baranis, one and a half twisting front from the stomach landing and some pupils have even completed triple twists from the back landing.

Back Kaboom (0.3)

Practise a low, slightly gained back drop to land, as shown in Figure 108a, the legs slightly raised from the bed. Upon landing, the legs are smartly beaten down on to the bed as shown by the dotted lines (Figure 108a). The hips are locked and the body will rise as in Figure 108b. Tucking the body, as shown in Figure 108c, will speed up the rotation so that it is easy to complete the rotation to the feet or stomach.

If any tension is lost in the body after the kick down to the bed, the rotational momentum will be absorbed in the body and the performer will find it difficult to complete the rotation. This can be a tricky move for some people. Support at the start by the coach holding the legs down until a strong rotation is felt can make the completion of this move easier.

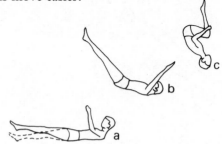

Figure **108** Back kaboom

6

Somersaults from the Feet with Twists

Barani (0.5)

The barani is possibly the move around which the idea of trampolining is built. It is a trampoline move in its origin and the move beyond which the great majority of performers never progress. It is a graceful move and is quite difficult to perform really well. Progress towards the barani comes via the front somersault with half twist. In the very early stages of trampolining the back drop with half twist is good practice for getting the right idea of the pace of the twist and the body shape for the barani.

Figures 109a–c show the body rising into the air with the arms well lifted and the twist beginning to show. The arms are held wide throughout the half twist (Figures 109d–g)

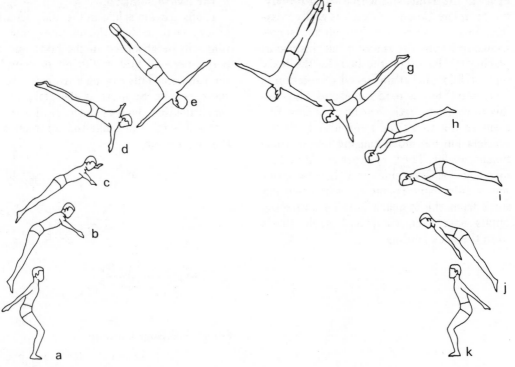

Figure **109** The barani

as shown or they can be pulled into the chest or placed at the side of the body. Performing the barani as shown in the figures, is good practice for the full and one and a half twisting front, since any wrapping in of the arms will result in rapid acceleration of the twist. The piking of the body, as shown in Figures 109h–j, will counteract any speed up of the twist caused by the arms being brought into the sides a little in preparation for the landing.

Many novices have a problem when learning the barani with pulling down at the take-off. In some instances this comes about because it has been learned from a cartwheel, in others because of excessive hip displacement and in others because of starting with the hands above the head, on landing, for the take-off. The take-off must be made with the

arms lifting well into the move, a strong leg push into the bed, and only enough hip displacement for the amount of somersault required. The body should be extended as the take-off is made rather than the idea of lifting the heels be pursued since this tends to lead to arching of the back in the twist.

Back Somersault Straight with Half Twist (0.6)

The back somersault straight with half twist is a very easy move on the trampoline and well within the capability of anyone who can perform the back somersault straight. There are two methods of performing the twist. One is an early twist commenced just after take-off and the other is a late twist started

Figure **110** Back somersault straight with half twist: method 1 using the early twist

just after the bed is sighted, the performer having just passed over the vertical upside-down position.

Figures 110a–l show the method using the early twist. The performer takes off as if for a back somersault straight and, as the take-off is made, the head is turned in the direction of twist to sight the bed (Figures 110a and b). As the body rises and rotates it is important to try to keep the eyes on the trampoline bed. At first this may prove a little difficult but only from a visual/psychological viewpoint. Once this technique is mastered (Figures 110c–f and j) the move becomes very useful, as a learning stage, in the progress towards the half in half out. As the body descends towards the bed the performer turns the head in line with the body for a normal front somersault-type landing. The

eyes are still kept on the bed so that orientation is retained; the landing is made with the head in line with the body and looking down at the bed (Figures 110k and l).

It may be necessary for some pupils to learn the easier method with the late twist. Like the full twisting back somersault straight, it is not the most useful method of performing the twist. From a normal take-off for a back somersault straight the performer must wait until the bed is sighted by the head being tipped back when the body is in the vertical upside-down position as shown in Figure 110e. The head is then turned sharply in the direction of twist and the rest of the body will follow. In practical terms the head and shoulders are turned but it does feel as if only the head is turned. Sight of the bed is momentarily lost but is regained for the

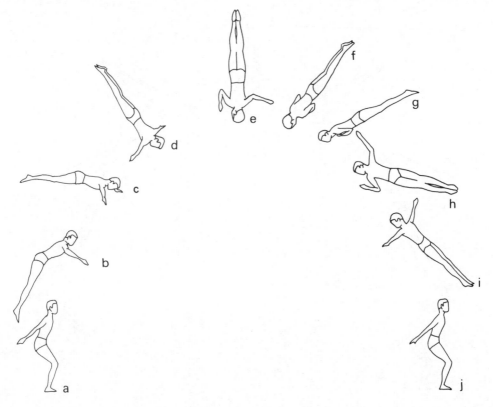

Figure 111 Front somersault with full twist

landing. Thus the complete half twist is carried out when the body is passing through the positions shown in Figures 110f–i.

It is very useful when this move is learned to practise it in the pucked position as a preliminary practice for learning the half in half out fliffus (*see* Figures 125 for the shape and an indication of the way in which the body is turned, initiated by the head and shoulders in the first somersault). As in the above skills it is important that sight of the bed is maintained throughout the somersault. Of course the somersault may be completed without sight of the bed throughout, but it does make orientation harder and may lead to problems later on in the learning of more advanced skills involving the half in start.

It is quite simple for the competent performer to add another half twist at the end of the move and thus to complete a late twisting back somersault straight with full twist. This may be useful for some pupils as a preliminary practice, but it is usually more satisfactory to learn the full twist as described in Figure 112.

Back Somersault with Full Twist (0.6)

The back somersault with full twist is one of the first advanced skills to be learned by many pupils. Good performance of this skill will be most useful for the better

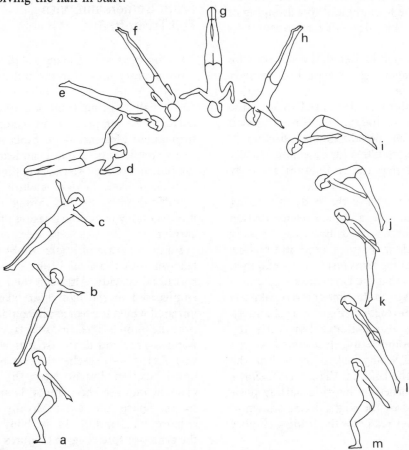

Figure **112** Back somersault with full twist

performance of all backwards twisting skills including fliffes.

Again, it is most important to keep the bed in sight throughout the whole of the skill so that the pupil is more relaxed than would be the case if there were loss of vision of the bed.

Figures 112a and b show the take-off and start of the twist. This is initiated whilst still in contact with the bed, with the arms wide and the eyes looking down at the bed. The push of the legs into the bed is strong, so that it is possible to let the body rise as one straight unit without any arching of the back due to dropping of one shoulder as the twist is set up. The eyes can be directed at an area quite near to the feet to avoid the temptation to look over the shoulders for the bed behind the back, which would lead to a dropping of the head backwards with consequent lean and travel.

As the take-off is started, try to make sure that the straight legs are pushed strongly away from the body in a forward direction whilst the buttocks are tensed to keep the trunk in a good straight line. Since this skill is usually the introduction to backwards twisting somersaults a lot of time is usually spent on getting the techniques correctly performed.

Figure 112c shows the body still rising with the arms wide and the eyes focused on the bed, which is now easily seen as the body turns towards it. Figures 112d and e show the wrap in of the arms just starting and then completed so that the twist speeds up and is practically over by the time the vertical position has been reached (Figures 112f and g). Figure 112g also indicates how early the twist is unwrapped and decelerated so that the pupil has a long look at the bed on the descent for the landing. Figure 112h shows the arms returned to the wide starting position followed by the slight piking shown in Figures 112i–k ready for the landing (Figure 112m).

The arms can also be pulled in to the sides of the body to increase the speed of the twist. This technique is preferred by some coaches. The half twist to crash dive is a good practice for this move, half twist jump into front somersault, layout back with half twist and any skill which will increase proficiency at twisting. First attempts at this move should be taken in the belt as described in the section on supports. At all stages it is important that the pupil only proceed if there is good sighting of the bed. Many problems with twisting somersaults stem from pupils learning the moves unsighted, which is quite possible but not in the best interests of the pupil if further progress is desired.

Front Somersault with Full Twist (0.6)

This move, as well as being a skill in itself, is a preparatory move for the full in half out fliffus. It is also a way into the rudolf or one and a half twisting front somersault. It is useful again for practice on seeing the bed throughout a forward twist. Since it is a relatively simple move a pupil can learn to vary the position of the twist during flight. It will be noticed that if the twist is a little late it will be difficult to see the bed throughout. Thus it is necessary to get the phasing of the twist correct.

Figures 111a and b (*see* p. 98) show the take-off with the arms lifting into the start spread fairly wide. Although the twist is not emphasised in the figures at take-off it is initiated whilst the feet are in contact. By the time the pupil has reached the stage shown in Figures 111c and d, the twist is well under way. As the body reaches the vertical upside-down position, but no later, the arms are brought into the chest smoothly and evenly to accelerate the twist already initiated (Figures 111f and g). As the body descends the arms are spread again (Figures 111h and i) to decelerate the twist ready for landing.

Figure 111i shows the body with the head still looking at the bed but slightly to the rear. The pupil must try to get the twist completed early enough so that the need to look to the rear is no greater than shown. If this happens the pupil will almost certainly land looking to the rear. The head should be in line and facing forwards for the landing as shown in Figure 111j.

The twist can also be accelerated by the arms being placed straight and in line with the side of the body. This will give a different timing to the acceleration; it is favoured by some performers. The twist in the pucked position is well worth practising for the full in half out fliffus preparation.

Front Somersault with One and a Half Twists (Rudolph) (0.7)

All work on the barani and full twisting front somersault is good preparatory practice for the learning of the front somersault with one and a half twists, usually called the rudi.

The main problem of the rudi is keeping the bed in sight so that the landing is easily and safely made. Many performers find that they see the bed, lose it, and then see it just before the landing. In this way they may have some slight difficulty in working from the rudi.

Figure 113 shows take-off from the balanced starting position without any forward lean and swinging the arms up and forwards with a certain amount of width between them and the shoulders turning slightly in the direction of the twist (Figure 113b–d). By the time the body is well up into the air about a quarter turn should be made with the arms still out wide (Figure 113e). This will represent the same position as the good straight barani. However, there is more twisting potential already put into the upper

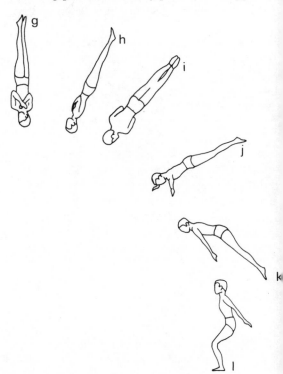

Figure **113** The rudolph (front somersault one and a half twists)

body. A very slight tilting back of the head enables the eyes to focus on the bed throughout the twist.

Figures 113f–i show the wrap up which increases the speed of twist. Make sure that it is not left too late or this may result in loss of sight of the bed, with consequent landing problems. Some people keep the head too much in line with the body and experience sighting problems. A simple experiment will show how little head tilt is needed. Tilt the head back until you can just see the ceiling. Turn the body through as many revolutions about the longitudinal axis as you like and

you will find that you can see the ceiling all the time. This is exactly similar to twisting upside down as far as your eyes are concerned. Figures 113j and k show the arms opening for the landing (Figure 113).

Leaving the twist too late also gives sighting problems and leads to landings with the body still twisting fast. The timing works out something like this: lift with arms wide, wrap in immediately on leaving the bed (even if it seems early), open the arms and pike for slowing up the twist and rotation in order to land under control.

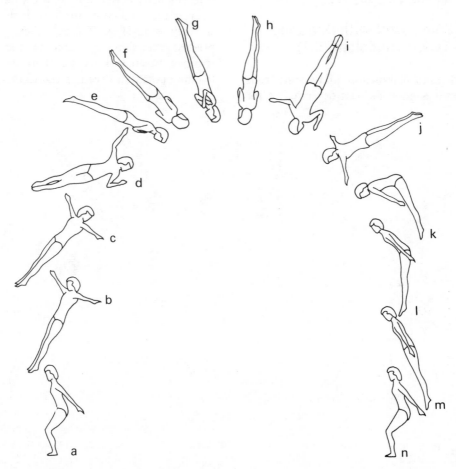

Figure **114** Back somersault with double twist

Back Somersault with Double Twist (0.8)

The back somersault with double twist is a skill which is often performed poorly because of a lack of tension in the mid-section of the body, and also because of poor phasing and lack of visual orientation throughout the move. First practise the back somersault with full twist with the arms well spread so that there is an acceleration potential built in. Make sure that the twisting power is initiated by turning the upper body from the waist upwards rather than by using the arms. If this is learned it should be fairly straightforward to accelerate from one to two complete twists. Start to turn the upper body whilst the feet are still in contact with the bed, and focus the eyes on the bed near the feet to help keep visual orientation throughout the twisting. Figures 114a–d show that the trunk is well twisted as soon as the body leaves the bed, and the waist is held straight and strong so that there is little possibility of movement out of the straight line so essential for good twisting. Figures 114e–h show the body with the arms in close, accelerated to complete approximately one and three-quarter twists. From that point Figures 114i–k show the arms opening wider, followed by a piking of the body to slow up the twist and to prepare for the landing (Figures 114l–n). Visual orientation is very important in this skill. As the take-off is started focus the eyes on the bed near the feet. As the body rises the gaze can be fixed on the same spot throughout the move (*see* section on visual orientation) and the bed will appear to move quite slowly enabling the pupil to see it clearly whilst in flight. This should help the pupil since there will be a more stable pattern, which is essential for calm well-phased skilful performance.

Assuming the pupil can perform a front somersault with one and a half twists, this can be used to progress towards the back with double twist. The procedure is as follows. Start as if about to perform a front with one and a half twists and turn a little away from the square position so that, in effect, the move will be a little more than one and a half twists. Progress a little at a time so that each step nearer to the double twist is only a small one. In this way the pupil does not have to build up too much determination to bridge the gap between one and a half and two twists. This, to the performer, is often a lot more to handle mentally than it may seem physically. The progressive advance also makes it easy to go back, if necessary, to a stage which the pupil can handle.

For many pupils it is good sense to use the belt and the crash mat at first. Remember that some performers who are trying multiple twists for the first time tend to fold up again just before they land and thus accelerate into the bed. It may happen because they have lost a little orientation or because they have concentrated on the new amount of twist so much that they have forgotten that a landing is needed. This problem seems to arise more with multiple twisting moves, both forwards and backwards than with other moves (*see* section on orientation).

Front Somersault with Two and a Half Twists (Randolf) (0.9)

The randolf, as the two and one half twisting front somersault is usually called, is one of those multiple twisting somersaults which is gradually disappearing from routines since the high number of twists and the problem of visual contact makes it less desirable to use than other types of skill with the same tariff.

To perform this move it is far easier to use the acceleration principle to its fullest advantage than to try to put in a high degree of early fast twist. The temptation is to give a good swing of the leading arm into the take-

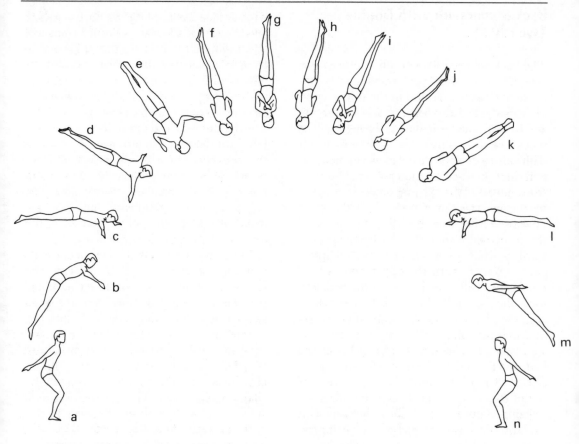

Figure **115** The randolf (front somersault with two and a half twists)

off in the mistaken idea that this action will make the twist better.

The twist must be started whilst in contact with the bed. Figures 115a–c show the take-off stalled a little and not showing too much twist as the departure from the bed is made. Figure 115c shows the twist with the arms well wide. Figure 115d shows the wide arms position still there, with the twist even further round. The eyes are obviously fixed on the bed to keep vision and to help aerial awareness. In both the front somersault with one and a half twists and two and a half twists, keeping visual contact with the bed is one of the major problems. Figure 115e shows the arms beginning to pull in to accelerate the twist to its highest speed of rota-

tion. It is important not to wait too long before the arms are brought into the chest (Figures 115f–j), since a late acceleration, although not affecting the amount or speed of twist, can affect the ability of the performer to maintain visual contact with the bed throughout the move. It also means that the performer will not be able to slow down the twist sufficiently to make a comfortable landing. This could be dangerous or it could affect the ability to get a good take-off for the next move.

By the time the position shown in Figure 115k is reached the performer is ready to slow down the twist before landing by opening the arms wide and beginning to pike (Figures 115l and m). The landing with arms ready for the next take-off is shown in Figure 115n.

Once again the important thing to remember about the learning of the front somersaults with multiple twists is that the twist must be started early enough to make sure that the bed can be kept in sight without having to bend the neck backwards too far, thus causing a tendency to arch the back. Even a small arching of the back can lead to some 'wobble' in the twist and loss of good form. This wobble is observed very frequently with many performers. It is caused partly by the head and partly by the lack of strength in the mid-section of the body. It is also caused to a certain extent by lack of knowledge of how to keep a straight body via isometric contraction of the whole middle of the body.

The visual problem, as in the one and a half twisting front somersault, is the same (*see* Figures 113a–l). The extra twist does make it necessary to twist slightly earlier than in the one and a half twisting front, but it must not be put in too early thinking of the extra full twist. There is a tendency to overturn this skill at first; this is counteracted by trying to get a little higher lift at the start and

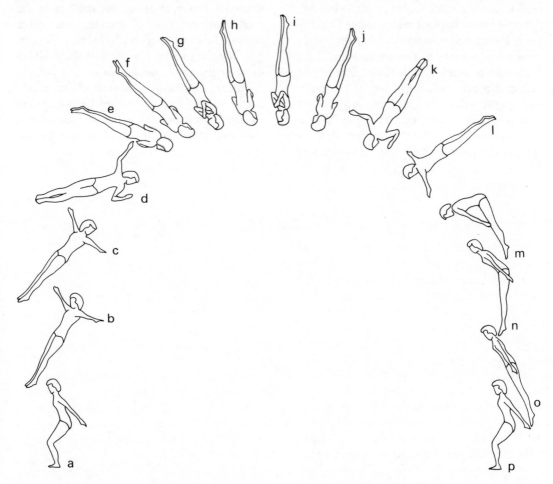

Figure **116** Triple twisting back somersault

'stalling' the take-off a little. The first attempts can be made in the belt although the very experienced pupil should find it easy to perform. Some pupils do find it difficult to cut back the twist to one and a half at first after learning the randolf. This will come back usually with a little more experience of both moves.

Triple Twisting Back Somersault (1.0)

Any pupil who can easily manage a good straight phased double twisting back somersault is mechanically able to generate enough twisting power to perform the triple twisting back. Practise first some double fulls with a good wide arm set up, making sure that there is no rush to accelerate the twist. Put on the belt and repeat this move to get the pupil used to the belt and to get him ready for the next step forward. Have also the crash mat ready for pushing in for the landing. Prepare the pupil psychologically for a smooth well set-up take-off so that the twist is not rushed. The belt should ensure that no harm will befall the pupil so that all the concentration can go into the set-up of the move, the pull in of the arms, and the small extra time scale of the hold in for maximum acceleration.

Look at the figures of the double and triple full and you will see that the triple full is very much the same for the set-up. There is then a faster wrap in possibly in practice a little earlier, a faster acceleration as a result and a come out at about the same phase of the total move. There is, at first, a tendency to hold on to the wrap for a little too long and also a tendency to forget about the landing in the total concentration of making the three twists. Only use the belt till the move is sure. Still use the mat for a while and above all try to keep the pupil calm. Watch out for the shoulders dropping at the start. As the number of twists increases do not allow any arm swing, which would increase somersault rotation, otherwise the landing will be unsighted and over-rotation will occur.

7

Multiple Somersaults

One and Three-Quarter Front Somersault Tucked (0.7)

This move should be learned with the aid of the harness and crash mat and not until the pupil has mastered a high controlled one and a quarter front somersault tucked with good drop out to a level landing (*see* support section for learning skills).

From a good height of jump, swing the arms forward and upwards, displacing the hips backwards at the same time and avoiding dropping the head and shoulders at take-off (Figures 117a and b). The body is then tucked tightly to get a fast rotation allowing an early extension of the body (Figures 117c–f). The body should be completely extended by the time it is horizontal (Figure 117g) so that a slowly rotating descent can be made with the body straight, needing only a slight bend for the landing quite high on the shoulders as contact is made (Figures 117h and i). This ensures that the landing is not overturned (Figure 117j). A good landing in the position shown helps

Figure **117** One and three-quarter front somersault tucked

to ensure that the following move is not travelled forwards and that good height may be generated by the rebound factor and the leg kick being in an upwards, not downwards, direction. An overturned landing results in the performer's legs being forced downwards on impact, giving a mechanically less advantageous take-off action.

The initial take-off from feet should be measured carefully to allow a long flight down for the landing. Work on this aspect only after a consistently safe landing has been mastered.

One and Three-Quarter Front Somersault Piked (0.8)

This move is very attractive to watch because it appears to rotate much more slowly than the tucked version. It does require a little more rotational power than the tucked

version, and also the pupil has a tendency to pull the move down instead of lifting it up. This occurs because of the anxiety of the pupil to get into the piked position.

It may be sensible for the nervous pupil to make the first few attempts at the piked shape in the rig or into the crash mat. One of the advantages in this move is that it is easy to break the piked position if the pupil feels that the rotation is a little slow. Bending the knees will speed up the rotation enough for the pupil to feel, and to be, safe.

Figures 118a–c show the move being well lifted without too much anticipation of the pike. Figures 118d and e show the well-folded pike with a low hand hold. Alternatively the pupil may hold the arms along the legs with the arms bent at the elbows. Figures 118f and g show the opening out with the straight position achieved just after the horizontal position. Figures 118h–j show a well-held descent and the gentle folding for the

Figure **118** One and three-quarter front somersault piked

landing ready to kick for height and perhaps further fast rotation on the rebound.

Double Back Somersault (0.8)

The double back somersault is probably the first double somersault most pupils learn. In many cases the move is attempted in the belt, with the pupil just being told to hang on to the back somersault having taken off with more power. If the pupil is lucky this may work and a double somersault may be performed successfully. However, getting round twice and landing on the feet whilst held by the coach and, by dint of many, many repetitions, getting the feel of the move so that the belt may be discarded is not a very progressive way to approach the teaching of this popular movement.

Most complicated skills are progressions from simple skills, and this is true of the double back somersault. The quality of performance and the power potential can be readily observed in a pupil who is preparing to try the double back somersault for the first time.

Sometimes it is suggested that the layout back somersault is a suitable preparatory move for those about to learn the double back. There are reasons why this may not be the case. The layout back tends to be performed by all but the most experienced performers with an arched back and the head tipped back. This would make it difficult for the pupil to tuck the body soon enough to make the double back a relatively simple move to perform safely. It might lead to a slowly rotating, fairly open tucked type of double back in which the pupil has to hold on to the tuck for a long time, thus landing whilst still rotating too fast for comfort or safety. The pupil who can perform the straight back somersault, with the head in line, is probably producing enough easy rotational power to be able to achieve a double back somersault

and still have time to land after opening out to slow up the rotation.

The development of power in the tucked back somersault is probably the easiest way to produce an easy double back somersault. The coach should be looking for a powerful arm swing, stopped at approximately shoulder height, a spotted back somersault without excessive dropping of the shoulders and excessive hip displacement forwards in order to stay on the spot, the head in line and a flying back somersault or open tuck 'armchair' body shape start to the back somersault. All the above should be performed out of the belt and only by a competent performer who can handle this type of work. It is important to realise that a double somersault should only be attempted by competent performers.

Any pupil having reached the above stage of development should be ready to move ahead. Check the amount of rotational power available by putting the pupil in the belt and performing the back somersault described above. Do not ask for great height at this stage, since it is important for the pupil to find out that great height and power are not needed. Ask the pupil, having taken off with enough power in the open tuck back somersault, to get round easily, without any further need to tuck tighter, and to repeat them a small number of times. Having observed that this is carried out easily, ask for a small amount of tuck to be added, but the pupil should still land on the feet, under control. One should be able to observe that it is only possible to start to tuck the body before it is necessary to straighten out in order to land on the feet under control. The pupil should feel a dramatic increase in the rotational speed as the body is shortened. Going from an open tuck into a tight tuck should produce at least twice as much rotational speed as is needed for the single somersault.

Now it is time to take the pupil verbally through the skill. If possible a demonstration by a competent performer of double backs will be very useful at this point so that the complete move can be seen by the pupil. It may be worthwhile to suggest that a little more power be put into the take-off, so that there is sufficient, and possibly a little more, than is needed.

The illustrations show the sequence of performance when attempting the complete move.

Figure 119a shows the strong arm swing being started with the body folded at the knees and waist but showing no lean. The head is in line. Figure 119b shows the arm swing stopped at about shoulder height so that as much of the rotational momentum as possible is transferred to the rest of the body. It also shows the straight leg drive, which may only be possible for the very expert performer, but which should be aimed for by all performers. This ensures that the body leaves the bed with a large proportion of the jumping and also rotational power being used, not being absorbed in a crumpled and slack body. Figures 119c–f show the body tucking to make the first rotation and then squeezing in still further to make the second rotation. The necessity to squeeze is due to the increase in rotational speed and the effect of centrifugal force. The performer will usually feel that a tight tuck is being produced even if the arms are not pulling a tighter tuck. This is because the extra rotational speed, continuing for a longer time, puts a more noticeable pressure against the hands than in the normal short time span tucking of the single back somersault. Figure 119f shows the squeeze. Some pupils freeze rather than squeeze. This gives a slow, even speed of rotation and the need to hold on for longer just to get round the second time.

Provided that a good squeeze has been achieved the speed will be sufficient to produce a good kick out due again to the effects of centrifugal force.

Figure 119g shows the performer just beginning to open out from the squeezed tuck. The head is tipped back to get an early sight

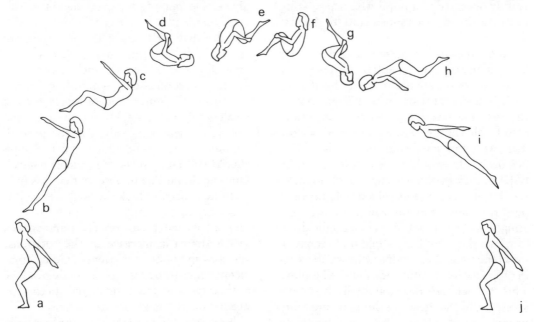

Figure 119 Double back showing the strong arm swing

of the bed, followed by a rapid straightening of the body which slows up the rotation quickly (Figure 119h). Figure 119i shows the body folding at the knees and hips ready for the landing on the bed with the body ready to commence the next jumping action or to stop (Figure 119j).

As the double back somersault is a very popular move, and brings the performer into the advanced category, it is very important to be able to recognise if the pupil is really ready to progress to this level. The preceding description gives a picture of the move in performance and related to the illustrations, together with the preparatory practices. It is necessary to give some space to the use of the belt and the crash mat for the first actual series of attempts.

First get the pupil to perform some open tuck back somersaults. Then go over the open tuck, plus the slight tuck, to get the feel of the sudden potential increase in the speed of rotation. Talk to the pupil about the whole move and the take-off with an increase in power plus the tuck squeeze open sequence. Instruct the crash mat operators, who should in any case be experienced, and let them have one go to reassure the pupil that they know what to do. Having gone through all the checks and preparation everyone should be ready to go ahead for the first attempt at the complete move.

Double Back Somersault Piked (0.9)

The double back somersault piked will follow naturally on from the double back tucked when the latter move has been well and truly established. It requires more power and has a much slower feel to it in performance. Learning is characterised by rushing the take-off, leaning back and buckling in the piked position.

Figure **120** Double back somersault piked

Figures 120a and b show a powerful start, the arms being swept through from behind the body powerfully and kept moving in an upward and forwards direction to add to the lift and to help the rotation. After take-off the pupil starts to pike the body (Figure 120c) and gets the fully piked position quickly to make sure that there is a good acceleration. The legs are pulled well in as shown in Figures 120d–g until about one and a half somersaults are completed.

At this stage the pupil will need to start to open out from the piked position so that the landing will not be overturned. Since this move has a slow feel to it sometimes the pupil holds on to the piked position too long. Figures 120h–j show the opening out for the landing with the final descent in Figure 120k.

Always perform first attempts at this move

in the belt. It is not a difficult move, but pupils tend to be unsure of the amount of rotation they have actually completed and vary between short and overturned landings. Using the belt allows small misjudgements to be corrected before attempting the move free.

Double Back Somersault Straight (0.9)

The double back somersault straight is one of the most spectacular moves performed; when performed well it has the appearance of grace, style, and power. It is a very powerful move and is attempted by the strong somersaulters only. This move should be attempted for the first few times in the rig so that the

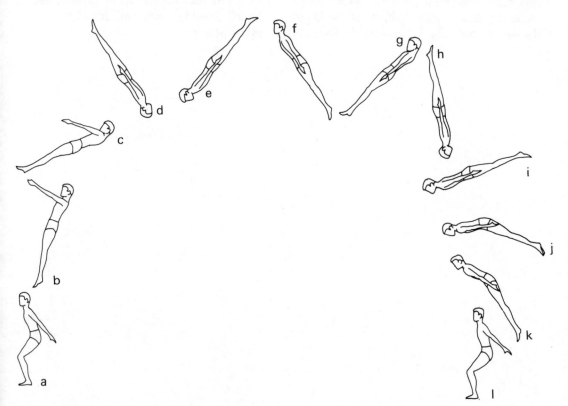

Figure **121** Double back somersault straight

pupil can get the feel of the move. There are no complications but it can fall a little short or feel as if it is not going all the way round.

Figures 121a–c show the start with strong arm actions, a good chest lift, and a straight body. At first the pupil will tend to arch the body excessively and force the head back in the attempt to get a more powerful rotational force. This will have a tendency to cut the height of the move and thus make it a little more difficult to attain the necessary rotation. Figures 121d–f show the body passing through the first somersault. By the time the pupil comes to the position shown in Figure 121g, there will be a feeling of easy completion or lack of sufficient rotation. If the former, continuation will be straightforward, keeping the body straight as in Figures 121c–g and continuing round as in Figures 121h and i, before piking in to land (Figures

121j–l). If there is a feeling of short rotation the pupil will rapidly pike or tuck the body by the time the position shown in Figure 121g is reached. Some pupils will find that they can keep good sighting and awareness all the way round by not tipping the head back at the start and by consciously keeping it forward as the second rotation is reached. This again will be for the very capable and experienced performer.

Two and Three-Quarter Front Somersault Tucked (1.0)

The two and three-quarter front is a move which should only be attempted by the most experienced pupils under the tuition of a very experienced coach. It is essential that the safety harness should be used (see Figure

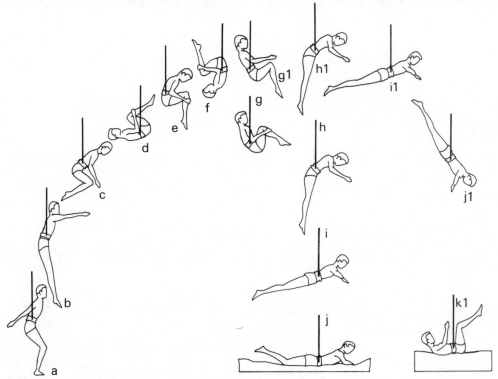

Figure **122** Using the safety harness for the two and three-quarter front somersault

122) until the coach and pupil are sure that the move is safely mastered. The safety mattress is also essential to cover any slight mistakes by the coach in the use of the safety harness. Both over and under rotation can be the cause of injury on this move. Removal of the crash mat means that any landing even with the harness in use will have more rebound than when the mat is there.

A reasonable sequence of learning could be *harness* and *crash mat*, *harness* without *crash mat*, *crash mat* without *harness* but with *coach* and *experienced spotter* standing on the frame ready to kill the rebound of the bed, if necessary. Only when the person responsible for the class, in consultation with the pupil, is sure that *all foreseeable risk* is removed should the pupil be allowed to try the move without harness, mat or coach standing ready on the side of the trampoline.

The most experienced pupils are those who can handle easily a number of fliffes in routine. A very experienced coach is one who has been coaching at fliffus and double somersault level for some time with success and without the need for supervision by a more experienced coach.

Having taken into account all the above conditions, the following methods can be used for teaching the two and three-quarter front. Using the harness and mattress, get the pupil to attempt the two and a quarter front somersault. The coach should bring the pupil down to rest on the mat as gently as possible to get used to the weight of the particular pupil and the point where maximum retardation must be applied. Having satisfied this requirement, and still using the harness and mat, the next stage would be to move ahead to the stage of the two and three-quarter somersault (see Figures 122h1–k1) overturned through the handstand position

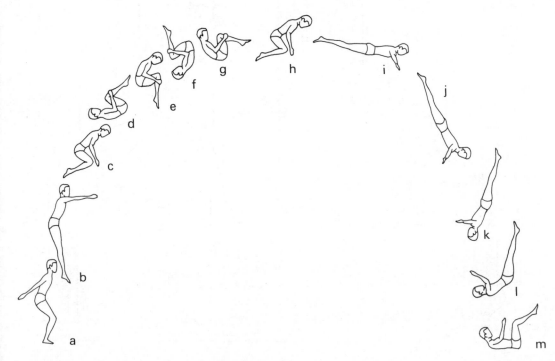

Figure **123** Two and one-quarter front somersault

to a gentle landing on the back of the mat. Once again this enables both coach and pupil to get accustomed to the extra rotation and the need to slow the descent and for the pupil to have the last part of the move in vision. As this part is practised the pupil usually becomes more confident and actually speeds up the move.

Make sure that there is no pressure on the pupil to move ahead quickly with this move since failure can be disastrous. Keep working for ease and sureness of performance. Some pupils will quickly get used to the extra rotation and will be able to handle each successive stage easily: however, even these pupils may have doubts at times and have to be coaxed along.

Once the pupil has the ability to make consistent landings the stages of the learning progressions can be covered until the pupil is able to perform the move without problems. One further situation may now arise–the pupil could, for some time, find that the one and three-quarter front presents a difficulty. This is a case of 'interference' and usually passes in a short time.

Many coaches insist that the pupil starts this move with the arms held high above the head and attempts to get the required rotation by pulling the arms down and flexing the body quickly. This may not be the best method of getting height and rotation but is a method often seen. Mechanically it may prove better to try to get an arms lifting action at take-off and to get the main rotational power from hip displacement (*see* Figures 123a and b), then use the tight tuck to accelerate the somersault. This method is more likely to enable the pupil to get a crash dive finish to the move than by pulling down at the start. (See Figures 123i–m).

Triple Back Somersault Tucked (1.2)

The triple back somersault tucked has rather lost its place as the move all good performers had to have in their repertoire. It has been superseded by the triffes, which are simpler to perform, although carrying a higher tariff.

The triple back should not be attempted unless the performer is secure in the safety harness. Needless to say, the person working the harness should be very competent at supporting fliffus and straight double somersaults and also two and three-quarter front somersaults.

At one time it was said that it was not wise to teach the triple back to any pupil who was unable to perform a standing double back. What this really indicated was that the pupil had to be able to initiate enough somersault rotation from a dead start to make the double back. Quite a good measure of the power needed at take-off is more easily obtained from the more powerful beds in use today. The real problem is in the awareness of the pupil in the measurement of the three rotations. It is not possible to see the way out of the move until it is, in effect, completed, as opposed to the forward two and three-quarter movements.

From a good starting position (Figure 124a) the arms are swung powerfully forwards and upwards, trying to make sure that they are not swung past the head causing backward lean, loss of height and travel. As soon as the take-off is made the arms reach for the knees and pull them into the chest (Figures 124b–d). If the head has not been thrown back too far it will be quite easy to pull a tight tuck of the body, making sure that there is no tipping back of the head before at least two complete rotations have been accomplished. It is also important that the physical sequence for the pupil is stated. Take-off, tuck, squeeze, hold, then release. Many attempts will be needed in the belt before the sequence and the power needed are learned by the pupil. Before the belt is removed both coach and pupil must be sure that each is confident of success. The move is straightforward, needs plenty of power,

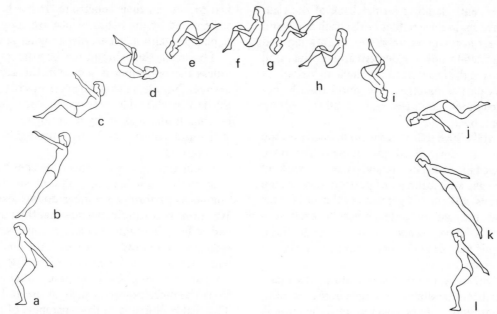

Figure **124** Triple back somersault tucked

needs the acceleration technique to be used and depends at the end on the correctly timed opening-out.

By the time the knees have been pulled into the chest (Figure 124d) the first rotation will have been half completed. Figures 124e–g show the performer most of the way through the second rotation. It may look as if the tuck is not too tight, but it must be remembered that at the speed of rotation in the triple back it is very hard to hold the knees tightly into the chest. The illustration shows

not the ideal but the normal level of performance. Figures 124h and i show the third rotation. Figure 124i indicates that the head is tilted back to see the bed for the landing and the necessary measuring of the landing position as shown in Figures 124j–l. If the opening-out were any later it would almost certainly result in an overturning of the landing. In a move of the power used in the triple back, an over-rotation could prove difficult to control and be dangerous.

8

Multiple Somersaults with Twists, Fliffes

Introduction – The Terminology of Multiple Somersaults

Within each sport there is some jargon which often serves to point out who are the knowledgeable and who are less so. In trampolining, however, many of the special words used are really a simplification of what could otherwise be some lengthy descriptions of quite complicated moves. Many of the terms are used universally, even being used by the Russians and Japanese in the English Form.

Much of the derivation is American and comes from various sources. A list of the terms appears at the end of this book, some of which must be learned by heart but others of which conform to certain simple rules of construction. The main group of these moves are included under the name *fliffus* (plural *fliffes*). This word means flip and twist. Flip is the American term for somersault and twist is as it says. Thus a fliffus is a somersault with twist. However, this term only applies to double somersaults and thus it is a double somersault with twist. Note that a single somersault with double twist does not come into this category although it is often written down as a double twister in casual description.

Having established the category of double somersaults with twists as fliffes, there is a need to go further to explain the system of distinguishing each type. This involves where the twist is and how many there are.

The twist or twists can be in either the first or second somersault or both and can range from one half a twist up to two and one half twists (to date).

Twists are described as 'half'–a half twist, 'full'–a full twist, 'one and a half' or 'rudi', 'double full'–a double twist, two and a half or 'randy' and 'triple full'–or triple twist.

The third classification is 'in' or 'out'. 'In' means that the twist/s are in the first somersault and 'out' means that they are in the second somersault. Thus a 'half out' is a double somersault with a half twist in the second somersault. A 'half in' is a double somersault with a half twist in the first somersault. In both cases the word half is often substituted by barani.

A 'half in half out' has a half twist in the first and a half twist in the second. The 'full in half out' has a full twist in the first and a half in the second, the half in one and a half (rudi) out has a half in the first and a one and a half in the second.

To the uninitiated the ins and outs of trampoline skills may be difficult to understand. A simple rule will help. In all skills of the fliffus type, total up all the twists. If the total is odd the move is a forward take-off and if the total is even the take-off is backward. Thus a full in half out is a forward rotating skill, and a back in full out is a backward rotating skill. Even with the above information it is only those in the fortunate position of being able to see advanced trampolining who will be able to recognise and name the whole range of fliffes instantly.

Barani Out Fliffus Tucked (0.9)

The barani out fliffus quite often is the first fliffus which is attempted by the pupil who is moving ahead into advanced trampolining. It is more easily learned by those who have had experience of the related moves like the tucked barani, the ball out barani and the one and three-quarter front somersault tucked. There would be no objection to anyone learning the barani out piked, except that more power is needed to perform the moves in the piked position and they feel as if they are being performed in slow motion compared with the tucked body position.

Familiarity with the moves mentioned above is really a prerequisite for the learning of the barani out. The one and three-quarter front somersault needs to be performed fairly high and with a fast rotation enabling the performer to open out and look at the bed before ducking the head under for the back landing. It might help if the pupil can spin the one and three-quarter front fast and let the last three-quarter front roll into the bed, looking for as long as possible at the bed, so that plenty of practice is experienced in awareness of the time-scale of the spin and the sighting of the bed with a view to adding a half twist at the end of the move. Whatever small differences are preferred, at the one and three-quarter front stage, it is important that the pupil can perform this move easily and definitely, seeing the bed well before the landing. A good test for ease of performance is for the pupil to follow the one and three-quarter front by another move of the ball-out variety.

Practise the barani tucked and the barani ball out trying to get as tight a tuck as possible so that the relationship with the fast spinning one and three-quarter front somersault is maintained.

Having worked at and consolidated all the

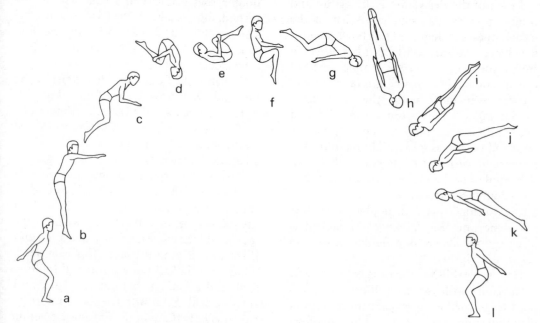

Figure 125 Barani out fliffus tucked

preparatory moves involved in the barani out fliffus there should not be much difficulty in performing the move in the belt. The two main problems which are likely to occur are under rotation and possible early twist so that the ceiling comes into the performer's view instead of the bed.

With the aid of the twisting belt and the crash mat it is time to make the first attempt at the move. Allow the pupil one or two further goes at the one and three-quarter front giving support at the opening-out stage so that there is a little more time for seeing the bed. The crash mat will be pushed in for these goes so that a slow rotation and short landing will not cause any major discomfort. Talk to the pupil so that a complete understanding of the timing of the twist and the extra speed of rotation is achieved and then make the first attempt at the whole move. The coach or the pupil may feel that it is better if the twist is called to the pupil. It may not be necesssary, but has the advantage of giving the pupil a signal to which to react and an indication of the length of time involved in the fliffus before the twist is added. Remember that the call must take into account the pupil's reaction time. Thus it is necessary to call some time before the actual point of the twist is reached. (See Figure 125g.)

Some pupils take-off and tuck up tightly so that they complete a double somersault to feet. Some open out too early and twist too early so that they see the ceiling instead of the bed. Some will open at the right time but will be rotating too slowly and will have to wriggle their hips over the top in the second somersault. The coach will have to be ready for all the above mistakes and hold the pupil safely in the rig. It should only take about three attempts for the pupil to see the bed and twist at the right time. If this does not happen fairly easily a little more preparatory work should be carried out. For instance the one and three-quarter front somersault may be a little too slow and the tuck being held too

long in order to get the feeling of enough rotation being present. This might cause the pupil to overrotate before coming out to see the bed and then finding that it is not possible to sight the bed before landing. It may be that the pupil is having to pull the hips and legs over the top for the barani in the second somersault. This again would be due to slightly slow somersault rotation so that there is a feeling of hip rotation as the legs are 'dragged' over the top and brought down to the bed. This hip rotation feeling is not present when there is sufficient speed of somersault rotation, since the twist comes easily as the body is straightened out over the top or even earlier to slow up the somersault speed for a gentle landing (see 125h).

Once the problem has been assessed, and the additional preparatory work has been carried out, let the pupil make some further attempts at the whole move.

The coach must make sure that the rig is used to help the attempts at the move. Give a little lift to the pupil to help overcome the weight of the belt and the slight inhibition felt at being strapped in. As the pupil comes to the end of the second somersault, carefully use the rig to slow him, if necessary, or let him drop into the bed without any deceleration from the coach. The crash mat should be pushed in for all the first series of attempts. The first weaning is the removal of the mat whilst still working in the belt. This gives the feeling of the harder landing whilst still in the control of the coach.

Barani Out Fliffus Piked (1.0)

Most pupils who have learned a competent barani out fliffus tucked will not have to go through a very long build-up to make an attempt at the piked version. Extra take-off power is needed to counteract the more open position of the body and hence the greater moment of inertia. There is a tendency for

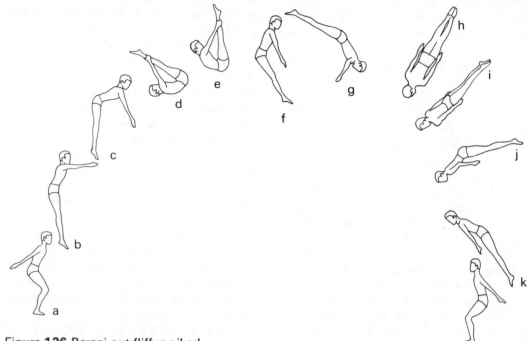

Figure 126 Barani out fliffus piked

the pupil to pull down at take-off trying to get more power; this must be avoided and the power should be taken from a more powerful use of the legs and slightly more displacement of the hips to put this extra jumping power into rotational power.

It is wise to try the first few attempts in the belt since the whole move definitely feels a little slower in flight than the tucked version. The pupil will also have a tendency to let the legs buckle in the second somersault in a reaction to a feeling of slower rotation. This can be corrected easily in the belt where the pupil will be more likely to hold on to the piked position than when performing free. A variation on the hand position shown in Figures 126d and e is to place the hands behind the lower calf and to align the forearms along the leg. This gives a better look to the piked shape.

Figures 126a–e show the normal take-off and piking. Figure 126f indicates an early come-out, with a good sighting of the bed in

Figure 126g before the half twist is initiated with at least half of the second somersault in the straight body position (Figures 126h–k). Performed in this way it is a good practice for the rudi out fliffus piked.

Barani Out Fliffus Straight (1.0)

This skill is one of those for the top class performer only. It was introduced by Stewart Matthews into his repertoire in 1980. It is only made possible because of the power available to the performer using the quarter inch beds with the latest type of springs. As an introduction to the move the pupil should be able to perform easily the one and three-quarter front somersault straight. Unless this move is within the grasp of the performer there is very little chance of success.

The real difficulty of this move is to produce enough rotational power to carry through the whole move without kinking the

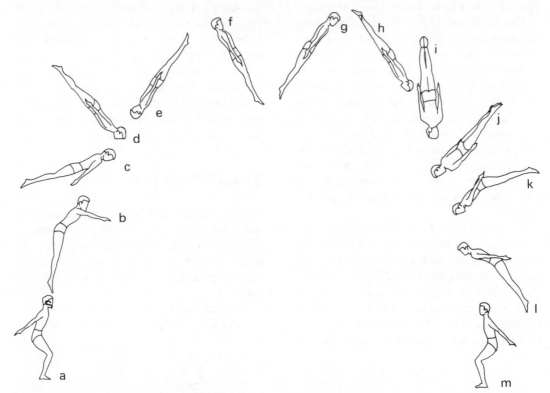

Figure 127 Barani out fliffus straight

body, especially at the end of the first somer-sault. Figures 127a–c show the powerful take-off with a minimum displacement of the hips and a straightening of the body as soon after take-off as is practically possible.

The next difficulty is keeping the head from dropping. Figures 127c–d show the pupil with the eyes focused on the bed whilst rising into the air. The critical stage of the whole move is now passing through the posi-tions shown in Figures 127f and g. At this point the pupil will feel either that the body position can be held or that there is a need to kink a little in order to make the double somersault. The straight descent and the preparation for landing shown in Figures 127h–m will come naturally if the previous stages have come right. With high level or very powerful moves the start decides the success of the rest of the move. Any straight

move is spoilt if the straight position is lost. Some pupils may like to try this skill in the rig at first if they are a little unsure of being able to produce the requisite power of rota-tion and a good height.

Barani In Tucked (0.9)

The barani in fliffus is an easy move to per-form. It sometimes seems harder to use than some other fliffes because of the acceleration at the end. The main requirement is a high straight barani (Figures 128a–h). The baby fliffus tucked will also help as a build-up skill. Overturned baranis will only be a use-ful practice if they are lifted well, kept straight for most of the flight, and then tuck-ed a little for the landing. If the overturned barani is pulled down it is not at all useful.

This move can be performed very elegantly.

The coach should give the signal at first to the pupil for the tuck. In this way the timing can be instilled in the pupil before the first attempt at the tuck and the whole move is made. Figure 128g indicates when the signal should be given. Figure 128h represents the time delay for the pupil to react. In this way the timing will be correct and not too late. Once the coach is sure that the pupil is getting the signal and the preliminary moves are sure, it is time to put on the belt and try the whole move (crash mat pushed in for the landing).

There can also be a problem from the point reached at Figure 128h, if the pupil has started the move with a very powerful rotation. On tucking the body (Figures 128i–k) the acceleration will be very fast, which may cause a loss of orientation and an overturned landing. Keep the start strong but not hurried. Work out the overall timing in the belt

and crash mat stage. From the stage shown in Figure 128i the move should be very like the baby fliffus. Watch also that the pupil does not start to tuck too soon, performing the last part as a side somersault rather than a back somersault. This move leads easily on to the barani in piked (Figure 129). Performed with an open tuck at the end it is good practice for the barani in full out fliffus.

Barani In Piked (1.0)

Having learned the barani in tucked it is quite easy to progress to the piked version. The effort needed in the second part of the skill is greater when piking than when tucking and produces a feeling of much slower rotation.

Start the move as for the tucked version but build in a little more rotational power to

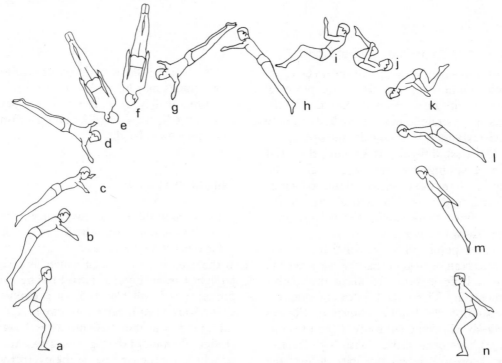

Figure **128** Barani in tucked

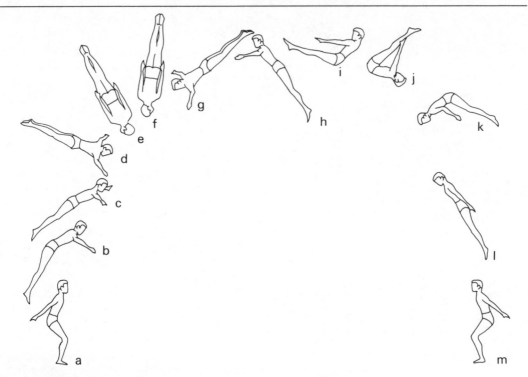

Figure 129 Barani in piked

cover the slightly slower speed of rotation in the piked position (see Figure 129).

At about the same position in the somersault rotation, or even a little earlier, pull in the legs strongly to the piked body shape. At first there will be a tendency to allow the legs to bend at the knees but this will soon disappear with practice. Try not to tip the head back as the legs are brought into the body.

Half In One and Three-Quarter Front Somersault Tucked (0.8)

The half in one and three-quarter front somersault tucked is the main progression for the half in half out fliffus. At first it is probably easier to try the move by starting with the shoulders already turned about one-eighth to one-quarter of a turn and the vision fixed at a point just behind the feet. The take-off can then be made as if for a normal

one and three-quarter front somersault. In this way there is very little problem about keeping the bed in vision. Gradually move the head round to the front and turn it as the take-off is made. The rest of the move is exactly the same as the one and three-quarter front somersault.

After some practice efforts should be made to perform the skill as illustrated in the Figures 130a–l. With a good lifted take-off and the eyes looking down at the bed turn the shoulders in the desired direction with a good spread of the arms (Figures 130a–c). As the body rises keep the bed in sight and let the body turn so that the twist is completed a little slower than in the earlier practice described above. There may be a little problem at this stage of keeping the bed in vision. It is important that the body is kept turning throughout the whole of the first somersault and that the half twist is completed as the first somersault is completed (Figures

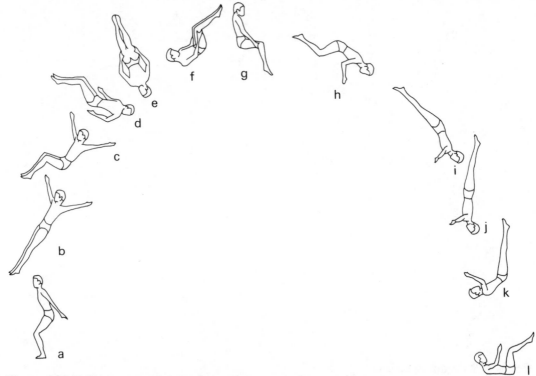

Figure 130 Half in one and three-quarter front somersault tucked

130d–g). The body should then be in the position shown in Figure 130g, facing directly opposite to the direction shown in Figure 130a. The body should keep on rotating as shown in Figures 130g and h in a slightly pucked position and should begin to open out to slow the rotation as shown in Figures 130i and j. The head is ducked as in Figure 130k ready for the landing shown in Figure 130l. Just before the landing is the only time when the bed should be lost from view and then only for a fraction of a second.

Half In Half Out Fliffus (1.0)

The half in half out fliffus is often the first fliffus where the 'pucked' position is used throughout the whole move. The double back somersault performed in the open or 'armchair' position is now a major require-

ment. Any arching of the back makes this skill more difficult and often leads to loss of vision in the middle of the move. The arching of the back can be a considerable problem with those who have a tendency to let the back arch at take-off. The pupil should practise the pucked double back in the belt to get familiar with the pace of the move and to learn the amount of power needed. The pucked half twist into duck under, watching the bed all the time, is also a very useful skill to have. The half in one and three-quarter front somersault is also a necessary move to have practised to land on the crash mat attempting to keep the bed in sight as long as possible in the early stages. The half twist into one and three-quarter front somersault should be practised until it is an easy flowing and sighted move. Cast at take-off should be corrected at this stage since it may be more difficult later on. The twist may be taken

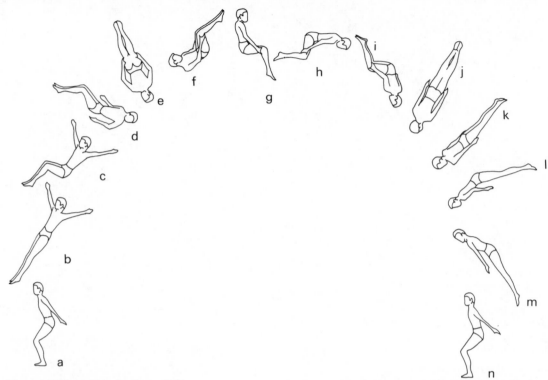

Figure **131** Half in half out fliffus

from contact with the bed, the more usual technique, or it can be initiated after take-off using the slightly pucked body position (RMI).

Figures 131a and b show the take-off with the twist already in the body just after take-off. The arms are still being used to aid the lift into the air. Figures 131c–f show the body beginning to puck (Figure 131c), the arms being brought down into the knees (Figures 131d and e) and the first half turn completed (Figure 131f). The first somersault is over by the position shown in Figure 131g. The performer should then be in a position (Figure 131h) to produce the second half twist. In the skilled performer this should flow evenly from the half in the first to the half in the second. However the learner may find that there are problems with insufficient rotation causing the last half twist to be started when the bed is not yet in sight or

there is a slight under-twisting causing the last part of the double somersault to be done in the side somersault position. To cure both these faults go back to the start and practise either with the rig or crash mat or both at the half in one and three-quarter front stage.

It is essential that the pupil is at the position shown in Figure 131h by the time that the second half twist is to be started so that the end of the move is as familiar as the end of the barani out fliffus. Figure 131i, still pucked and twisting, leads into the straightening out of the body and completion of the twist (Figures 131j and k). There is then a slight piking of the body for the landing (Figures 131l–n).

This move can be tricky if the basics of preparation are not conscientiously practised, particularly if the pupil is badly unsighted. It is a direct lead into the half in one and a half out fliffus.

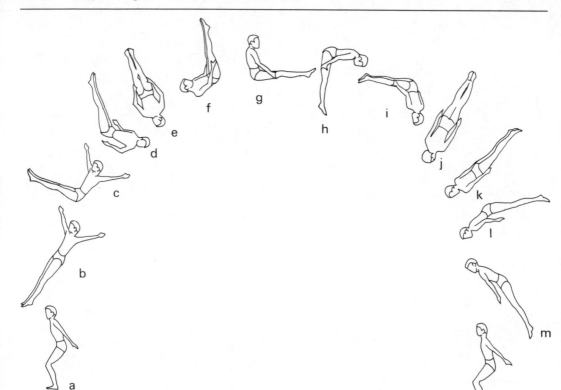

Figure **132** Half in half out piked

Some pupils may find that they can easily initiate the twists after the start of the somersault when the body is in the pucked position using RMI techniques. This is acceptable and definitely avoids the dropping of the leading shoulder often seen when the twist is initiated whilst in contact with the bed. It is, however, not the more generally used method.

Half In Half Out Piked (1.1)

This move is not a very beautiful move since it is often done in such a way that the transition from straight, just after take-off, to piked can be poorly phased.

Figures 132a and b show the take-off with the body straight just after leaving the bed and the arms fairly wide (Figure 132c). The twist has already been put in during the take-off, keeping the bed in sight. As soon as the body is well clear of the bed the legs are brought in straight towards the body and the body will move down towards the legs. The twist should be a little stronger than for the tucked half in half out, since the extra length of leg will resist rotation a little more. The arms will move down to grasp the legs between the upper thigh and the calf in order to help keep a strong hold on the piked position (Figures 132d–f).

Every attempt to keep the bed in sight should be made during this move but it may happen that sight will be lost at the point shown in Figure 132f as the body completes the first half twist and almost completes the first somersault. As the body completes the first somersault and moves into the second (Figures 132g and h) sight is easily regained and the final phase (Figures 132i–n) is exactly the same as for the half out piked.

This move is used usually where there is a need to increase the difficulty of a routine and to avoid repeated skills or loss of difficulty. It may not get very high form marks because of the difficulty of presenting the move in a clean, clear-cut way.

Double Front Somersault Tucked with One and a Half Twists in the Second Somersault (Rudi Out Tucked) (1.1)

The rudi out fliffus is regarded as one of the more difficult fliffes. This may be because, if the front somersault with one and a half twists is not learned well, problems will arise when it is put into a fliffus. The following skills well learned will be an advantage before attempting the rudi out: ball out barani straight, rudi ball out, one and three-quarter front somersault with very early 'kick out', barani out with an early 'kick out'. All these moves need a high degree of rotational power to get the early 'kick out' or the straight held position in flight.

The pupil should also be used to a well sighted one and a half twisting front somersault. Many pupils have learned the one and a half twisting front somersault without seeing the bed all the way through the move and often experience some difficulties with the landings. This problem can be transferred to the fliffus, causing landing problems. Corrective work should be undertaken early.

Two approaches can be made to the 'rudi out'. The first is to use the barani out as a starting point and try gradually to roll the barani on to complete a full twist. This can be done easily by a pupil who has mastery of the barani out. Pupils who can also easily

Figure **133** Rudy out tucked

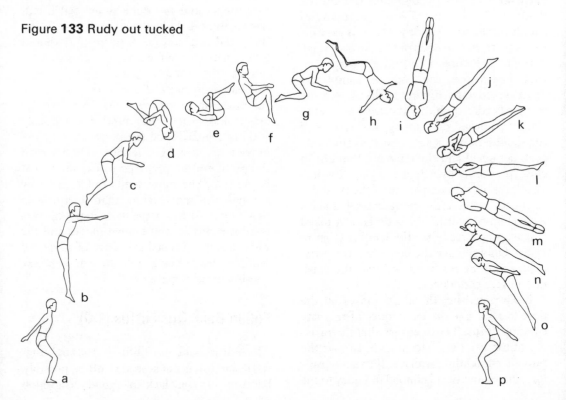

perform a front somersault with full twist should have no difficulty in achieving the full twist stage. There is no need to use the belt up to this stage. It will now help if the pupil practises one and three-quarter front somersaults to establish a full extension from the tuck as soon after 360° as possible, to give a good long look at the bed before landing.

Put the pupil in the belt and go for the whole move. It may well be that the pupil will lose sight of the bed during the last part of the fliffus for the first few attempts. This will probably be because the twist has been started too late, possibly because of too slow a rotation over the whole of the somersault. Go back and work on the take-off ensuring that there is no pull down at the beginning in the anxiety of seeking fast rotation.

The second approach is to put the pupil in the belt and try the whole move into the crash mat. Figures 133a–c show the good open take-off not rushing into the tucked position. A tight tuck (Figures 133d and e) speeds up the somersault so that it is easy for the pupil to start to open out as the 360° stage is reached (Figures 133f and g), starting to twist just before the body is completely straightened out (Figure 133h). It can be seen in Figure 133h that the twist is created from the pucked position by the twisting of the shoulders and is accelerated as the body is straightened and the arms are brought in close to the body (Figure 133i). Figures 133j–m show the completion of the twist decelerated by the arms being extended sideways (Figure 133n). The body is then piked (Figure 133o) ready for the landing (Figure 133p). Only remove the belt when the pupil is judged to be ready but still use the crash mat to give confidence.

Keep practising the allied moves all the time to reinforce the techniques of this late twisting fliffus. Try to ensure that the phasing of the twist is early enough, so that the pupil is not landing whilst still twisting rapidly, increasing the likelihood of injury to the ankles and knees. This move when learned becomes the way in to the half in rudi out and the full in rudi out.

Double Front Piked with One and a Half Twists Out (Rudi Out Piked) (1.2)

The preparation for this move is not as elaborate as for the rudi out tucked. By the time a performer has reached the level of skill required for the rudi out tucked it is easy to switch to the piked move. It is still useful to be able to perform the barani out piked and the ball out barani and rudi ball out piked as aids to awareness for the rudi out piked. They are not all essential but will be helpful.

It must be remembered that a piked move does take a little more rotational power than the corresponding tucked move. Provided that the pupil can handle the above preparatory moves and has done some well lifted, fast rotating early kick out barani out fliffes, the piked rudi out (see Figure 134) should follow naturally. However it is always safer to make the first attempts in the belt. Once this has been successfully accomplished try the move on to the crash mat. Remove the crash mat when the pupil is obviously making regular good landings, and try the move to a normal bed landing. Do not rush the pupil and be prepared to use the mat if requested. The pupil tends to feel the way through this move rather than learn it as a new move. At this stage most new skills are combinations of well-known moves and the pupil has not reached this stage of advanced work without being able to put complex combinations together.

Full In Back Out Fliffus (1.0)

The full in back out fliffus is a straightforward skill but is not seen very often, possibly because of the lack of good technique

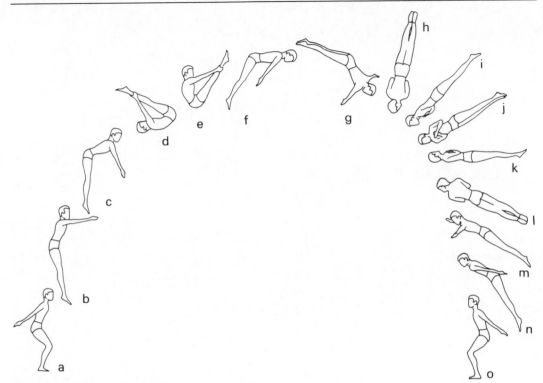

Figure **134** Rudy out piked

sometimes shown by some performers. There is the added problem of the sudden speeding of rotation at the end of the move. Any arching of the back in the first somersault will also tend to make the skill a little unsure.

First of all, the pupil must work on a full twisting back somersault which is high and straight. Any arching of the back at take-off will tend to cause a wobble in the full and tend to cause loss of height and power. Make sure that the full twisting back is straight, that the twist is finished well ahead of the drop-out, and that the pupil does not need to pike in to land. Practise the first part with height and straightness, and let the pupil know that there is plenty of time to carry out the second part only when there is ample visual evidence of sufficient power in the first somersault to be able to tuck up tightly for

the second complete tucked somersault. The fact that the first somersault can be performed straight is a good indication that there is likely to be enough rotation for the second somersault when the body is tucked up.

It is a good idea for the pupil to be able to carry out double back somersaults in the open tuck position holding that position throughout the two somersaults. This indicates that the pupil can develop enough power to cover a straight, and a tucked, somersault in combination. Use the crash mat and let the pupil practise some full twisting backs and carrying on round to a flat back landing on the mat.

It is now advisable, if it is thought that there is sufficient power, to try the move in the belt. Very few people can handle this move at a first attempt and remain totally aware of their whereabouts in space.

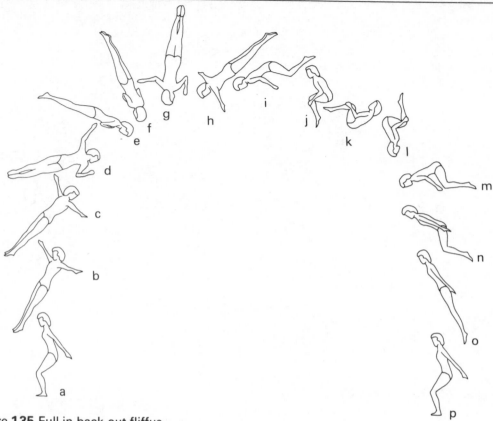

Figure **135** Full in back out fliffus

Looking at Figure 135, the position of the body in Figure 135i shows how early the performer has to think of the tuck. It is really almost as soon as it is realised that the full twist has been completed. There is a tendency for the pupil to want to tuck early, so early that there is a chance that the second somersault will be a side somersault. It is the responsibility of the coach to let the pupil know when the full twist is finished by some verbal indication. This must also be practised in the belt. Work on this until both coach and pupil are happy that the tuck can be pulled in at the right time. If the full twisting part is high and straight even a half-hearted tuck will get the pupil round. Practise in the belt until the whole skill is going well, then remove the belt and work onto the mat. It is always wise at first to work up to

subsequent attempts at moves of this level in each session. The Figures show the full well lifted, and sighted, and completely finished before the tuck starts in the position shown in Figure 135i.

Back In Full Out Fliffus (1.0)

The back in full out fliffus is not a move which pupils will move on to on their own; it has to be taught. In learning this move, as with all backward fliffes, the open or pucked double back somersault is a very good preparatory skill. It shows that the successful pupil has enough power to be able to complete the move with one somersault open and one tucked.

Plenty of practice on the double back

pucked is useful at all times. Move on to the pucked back somersault with half twist to stomach on to the crash mat. Work on this until it is high and easy with a drop out to the stomach. It should be performed with a definite open out to an almost straight position well before the landing rather than holding on to the pucked shape until a landing is made. Do not move ahead until a good height is obtained throughout this part; it will tend to be low and fast at first.

The next stage is to put on the belt and go over the above into the mat and then try to move on to the next stage overturning the stomach landing to the handstand on, or above, the mat. Try to raise the height of the move, with a more vertical take-off until it is

possible to come out into the handstand position three or four feet above the mat. By the time that this stage has been reached it will probably be easier to complete the whole move than to carry out the last progression.

Figures 136a–c show the standard take-off for a double back with tuck opening out quite early in the first somersault (Figures 136e–g). As the body reaches about 360°, or even slightly earlier, the twist is started (Figures 136h and i). If there is enough twisting power from the head and shoulders being turned as shown in Figures 136h and i, the full twist should flow easily round. If this does not happen it may be necessary to use a tucked front ending to the move. A sharper turn of the head and shoulders should rectify the

Figure **136** Back in full out fliffus

problem: the turn should be started as the body reaches the position shown in Figures 136f and g. At this point the pupil should be concerned with keeping the bed in sight as the twist takes place, especially during the section shown by Figures 136j–l. The final descent to the landing is shown in Figures 136m and o. The arm position as shown may be modified so that the arms are by the side during the completion of the twist. It does give a slightly sharper acceleration to the twist but is not necessarily going to gain more marks from the judges.

One of the major problems with this move is starting the full twist too early so that the move becomes a late half in half out. On a number of occasions incorrect phasing of this move has led to coaches or team managers protesting that a routine included a repeat and thus the tariff value should be lost. More time spent on the correct phasing of this move, with the full twist not starting until the come-out from the first somersault is taking place, will help your pupil avoid losing tariff marks in this way.

Full In Full Out Fliffus (1.2)

This move is related to the full in back out and the back in full out fliffes. Those performers who have mastered both the above fliffes should have no real difficulty in completing the full in full out. Once again they should be able to perform the double back pucked easily, indicating plenty of power in a double rotation in a fairly open body position. The two fliffes mentioned above also demonstrate the ability to set up a twist at the beginning of a double somersault and to perform RMI twists in double somersaults.

It may be necessary for the pupil's confidence to go through some repetitions at the full in one and a quarter to back drop followed by a further half twist to stomach at the one and a quarter stage. These can be carried

out in the belt or free, depending upon the ability of the pupil. If either pupil or coach has doubts, work in the belt with landings on the crash mat.

After some practice at the full in one and a quarter with half twist to stomach it should be possible for the pupil to attempt the duck under instead of the stomach landing. At this stage make sure that the start is well lifted, as shown in Figures 137a–c, with the twist and puck coming in together. Figures 137d–h show the completion of the full twist and the first somersault. From the position shown in Figure 137h the pupil could drop down to the back drop landing on the mat and supported in the belt, when learning. The position shown in Figure 137i shows the half twist ready for the stomach landing using belt and crash mat. The next progression could be to the position shown in Figure 137j ready to duck under for back landing. The arms would have opened out to slow the twist.

If the pupil is able to get as far as the position shown in Figure 137j and then duck under, with good timing, it should be relatively easy to progress to the last part with the final half twist as shown in Figures 137k and l. The landing is shown in Figures 137m and n.

All the way through these advanced skills, it may be necessary to work for some time on consolidating each part. It may seem to the coach that the skill is coming easily, but the pupil may have mental problems which will interfere with progress. Make sure also that the skill is sighted. Many pupils, especially when young, may handle unsighted skills, even advanced ones, but there often comes a time when it can start to get frightening. Teach seeing the bed.

At first this skill may be jerkily performed as far as the twist is concerned, but, given time and patience and the development of skill, the two twists should run easily into one another.

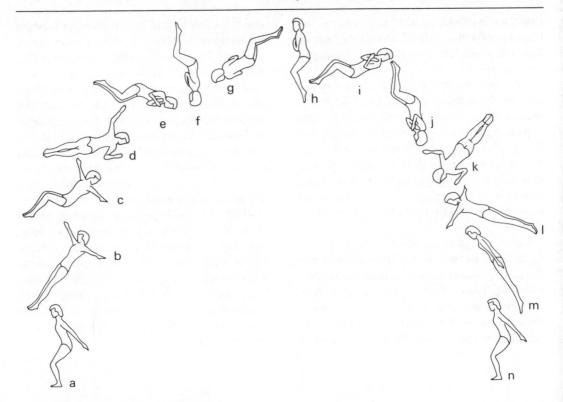

Figure **137** Full in full out fliffus

Full In Half Out Fliffus (1.1)

The full in half out fliffus is one more form of one and a half twisting double front somersault. It is normally performed in the pucked position, but can also be performed straight by the most skilled performers. The pucked position is used to enable the somersaults and the twists to be of such a speed as to allow the performer to see the bed throughout. For many performers a new skill has to be learned, the pucked full twisting front somersault with the bed in sight throughout. This move has a totally different feel from the straight twisting front somersault. It is useful also to practise the pucked one and three-quarter front somersault. This requires quite a lot of power and there is no need to think about the timing of opening out

for the landing: the pupil just lets it roll round into the bed.

To reach tariffs of 10.00 or more, the full in half out is usually one of a number of fliffes needed. To perform fliffes with twists in each of the two somersaults, a good skill vocabulary is needed. In this instance mastery of the full twisting front somersault is necessary. It should be practised to feet and to front drop landing. Make sure that the drop is from a good height and not just scraping into the bed, to prepare the pupil for the duck under to make a full twisting one and three-quarter front somersault.

Before attempting the full twisting one and three-quarter front, put on the belt and get the crash mat ready. From the full twist to handstand take the move to the handstand position just as for the one and three-quarter front. Keep practising until sure that the full twisting section is sighted. In this way a good base for a sighted start is being developed and consolidated all the time.

The full twisting one and three-quarter front is the difficult part of this fliffus, but once that is mastered the end should be easy to put on since it is the end of the barani out fliffus. It is imperative that the pupil is not forced to move on too quickly; this could lead to problems with losing sight of the bed and getting lost. Keep practising until the pupil feels ready to move into the next part without qualms.

Figures 138a and b show a good lift into the move. The twist is started on the bed and the puck position begins to take shape after take-off (Figure 138c). Figures 138d–f show the somersault and twist coming to completion just as the somersault reaches full height. For the learner the first somersault

and full twist should be complete, at least by the attainment of full height (*see* Figure 138g).

From the position shown in Figure 138g, if there is enough rotation, the pupil should find it easy to complete the final twist (Figures 138h–k). Figures 138l and m show the descent for the landing with plenty of time and space. The beginner may find at first that the move is performed short of rotation. Do not let him rush the start but concentrate on a good easy lift of the arms without lean or dropping of the head.

With this skill, progress in small stages only. If there is a problem move back a little and then try to move forward again. Go from the belt and mat, to mat, to stand, to completely free. Take care, and remember that for most pupils this is a new departure in trampoline skill. Loss of confidence at this stage may cause a major hold-up in tariff development.

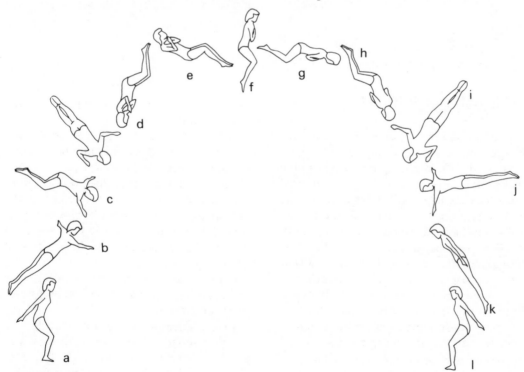

Figure **138** Full in half out fliffus

Full In One and a Half Out Fliffus (Full In Rudi Out) (1.3)

This fliffus is related to the full in half out in the same way as the barani out is related to the rudi out. Basically it should not be attempted until the full in half out is mastered and usable in routine. By the time any pupil has reached the level of rudi out and full in half out, progress is often just a matter of attempting one of the variations on a skill already established.

Make sure that the full in half out has plenty of height and that the half out is straight and performed with ease. The pupil may prefer to make the first attempts in the belt or may feel that the move is easy to perform free. If there is any chance of the pupil getting lost or there is a history of some

sort of orientation problem with the rudi out the first attempts must be made in the belt.

Make sure that the take-off (Figures 139a–c) is lifted, not dropped down. The pucked position should be held throughout (Figures 139d–i) so that the full twist is not too fast and so that the one and a half twists may be taken from the pucked position shown in Figure 139i. This permits plenty of twisting power to be initiated as the body begins to straighten. Normally the twist is very fast in the second somersault (Figures 139j–l); it should not be too low, or the pupil will still be twisting fast as the landing is made. As in all forward twisting somersaults it is far better if the bed can be kept in sight throughout the twists, especially for the landing with the twist slowed by the arms being widened (Figures 139m–o).

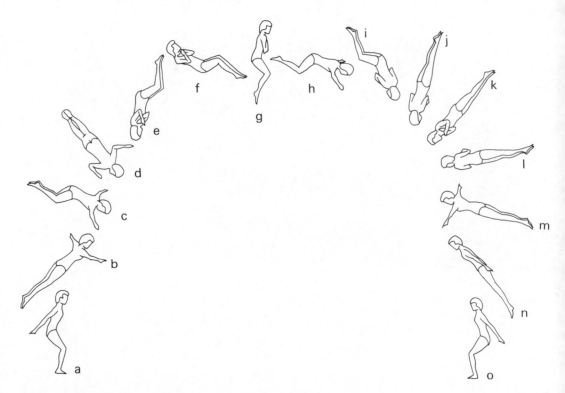

Figure **139** Full in rudy out

Half In One and a Half Twisting Front Out Fliffus (1.2)

This move, more commonly called the half in rudi out, is really just a combination of the half in half out and the rudi out. However it is not wise to try it until both the above mentioned moves are well handled by the pupil. It is safest to try the first attempts in the belt, since most pupils tend to rush the half in start and thus have less time for the hard part at the end.

As for the rudi out, some fast half in one and three-quarter front somersaults, with a good early stretch out to the straight position, set the somersault pattern for the move.

Follow this with a series of rudi out fliffes if possible with an open pucked position for the first somersault which will approximate to the body position during the half in start to the move. In this way the pupil can get as near as possible to the feel of the move in both halves before attempting the whole move.

Once both coach and pupil are satisfied that no more in the way of build-up to the move can be done, put the belt on and try the whole move. Figures 140b–d show the well-lifted early twisting start. Figures 140e–h show the mid-part of the first somersault with the hands held under the thighs in the pucked position. Although the move should

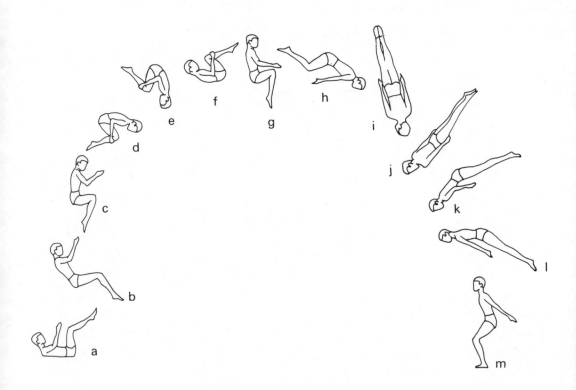

Figure **140** Half in one and a half twisting front out fliffus

not be rushed, enough rotation must be obtained by the time the pupil has reached the position shown in Figure 140i to give enough time and space to make the one and half twists down to the landing. Good preparation work will pay off, as in all multiple twisting fliffes. Confident successful repetition of this move is necessary before the belt is removed and the first free attempts are made into the crash mat. If there is loss of confidence put the pupil back in the belt for a few more attempts and try the move free again.

Double Ball Out with Half Twist Out (Ball Out Half Out) (1.0)

This move is actually a two and a quarter front somersault from the back landing position. The extra quarter somersault comes at the start. The move presents a certain amount of more difficulty than the double ball out, which is comparatively easy. The double ball out is a required move before attempting the ball out half out.

Even if the pupil is performing the double ball out easily, it must be high and with a

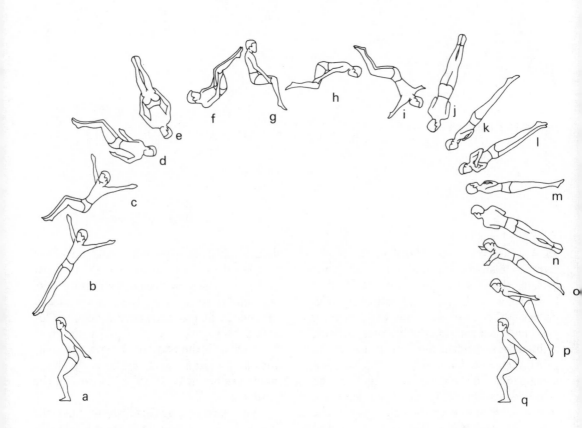

Figure **141** Ball out half out

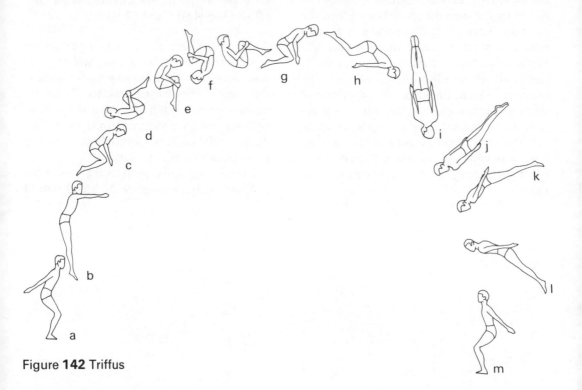

Figure **142** Triffus

good sighted come-out. Many pupils do perform low fast rotating double ball outs and, because there is the possibility of landing high or low on the back and still being safe, do not bother to progress further. To get a good high fast rotating double ball out with sighted come-out, the pupil must master the initial vertical kick into the air as the rotation is initiated. This gives added height to the move and consequently added rotation time. The kick helps to keep the body open at the start as rotation begins (Figures 141a–c) and this helps the pupil to produce acceleration. The tight tuck comes in in the early middle phase of the move (Figures 141d–f), which is about the highest part of the whole skill. The tuck is released in preparation for the half twist out as the body becomes upright for the first time (Figure 141g), the legs are kicked out and the longitudinal twist is begun (Figure 141h). Figures 141i and j show the twist finishing with the body in the straight position, and Figures 141k–m show the body piking to stop the twist and to prepare for the landing.

This move is a good finishing move for those who are getting up to tariff levels of 8 and above. It is also a preparation for the more difficult ball out rudi out.

Triple Front Somersault with Half Twist Out, Tucked (Triffus) (1.3)

Trampolining has progressed so far recently that two and even three triple somersaults are being performed in routine. These triple somersaults are normally with twists and are called 'triffus' in the singular form and 'triffes' in the plural form. It is a combination of triple and 'flip' ('flip' meaning somersault).

Before any performer is expected even to think about practising this skill, he needs to have a very high level of consistent performance on double somersaults with twists and also the two and three-quarter front somersault. The above moves must be out of the belt, fit to be used in routines, and performed not only consistently but with power to spare.

It is highly dangerous to let any pupil try any first attempts at the triffus out of the belt. It is also wise to use the crash mat in conjunction with the belt.

A similar procedure as for learning the barani out fliffus can be adopted. The pupil puts on the twisting belt and is supported for a number of two and three-quarter front somersaults with an early extension to a supported descent in an open body position either to back landing or to feet. Since the pupil already knows the barani finish at the end of the barani out, it should be straightforward to add that ending to the two and three-quarter front, when supported for the landing. Before the pupil tries the move out of the belt and on to the crash mat both coach and pupil should be completely prepared.

9

Physics Definitions; Principles of Motion; Illustrations of Principles

These definitions are intended to help the coach and the pupil to understand, in some small measure, the principles which apply generally to movement of bodies on the trampoline and in the air. It is not intended to substitute for a serious study of physics or the mechanics of human movement but, if read carefully and understood with the aid of the Figures, it should give a basis for the acquisition of a working knowledge of mechanical factors involved in trampolining.

It must be realised that the human body is a mobile object and not a rigid object and that, although the principles applied to it mechanically do work, maximum efficiency is only possible when the correct amount of body tension is applied for the purpose desired. It is also true that we are all constructed with many differences in weight, strength, proportion, leverages and mobility, and thus each individual will move in a slightly different way from any other, and will be affected by other personal characteristics. Some people move in a smooth way and others in a jerky way from the beginning. This may be one person's natural advantage over another. Knowledge of mechanical principles should help the interested to avoid some of the more disadvantageous mechanical faults.

The figures used are, wherever possible, taken from the trampoline skills so that they may make for better understanding of the application of the principles to trampolining. More than one figure may be used to illustrate one principle. It must also be remembered that a number of principles will often be in operation at the same time since they are interelated and interdependent.

Whatever methods of teaching skills on the trampoline are used, all those involved must realise that any actions which do not purposefully use the correct mechanical principles will lead to less efficient performance. This must not be mistaken for a judicious balancing of the effects of two or more opposing principles in order to obtain a specific effect. For example, a coach may allow a pupil to lean into a forward take-off in order to get enough rotation to perform a one and three-quarter front somersault. He is prepared to accept travel and loss of height in order to achieve success in the move. However, the end product is not as good as it would have been if more time had been spent on the correct techniques, according to the best mechanical principle for that particular move, instead of accepting less good performance to save time. Furthermore, even the time is not really saved, as further time will probably be needed to correct the faults allowed to develop.

Many of those involved in the teaching of sport are too ready to take up 'the latest idea' rather than sticking with good mechanics until that idea is either proven or disproven.

This unfortunately affects the pupils, who have to try to progress under greater difficulties than necessary. The study of mechanical principles will help both pupil and coach to approach efficiency better than the mere following of fashion.

The three basic laws of motion as defined by Sir Isaac Newton are the basis of the principles of motion which are used by those involved in the study of motion, which means coaches and pupils. Any actions which are proposed by a coach should be soundly based on the simple principles. If the movement is a complicated one it is still derived from simple principles. It should be possible to trace any movement to simple laws of motion. If this cannot be done then some questioning of its soundness is necessary.

As mentioned earlier it is sometimes necessary to sacrifice the effects of one principle to obtain a desired effect at the expense of another basic principle. What cannot be done is to overstress one principle without loss of another. Again it must be realised that some extremely capable performers have been very successful in spite of the use of unsound techniques. It may have been decided that to change the whole technique might have been too long a time scale to enter upon and still keep the success of the performer constant. Relearning may have spoiled the total combination of skills the performer had and may have been less advantageous in the long run.

The law of inertia

The first basic law of motion is that of inertia. Inertia is the resistance to any change related to motion in a body. Any change of motion —starting, stopping, accelerating, decelerating or changing direction—requires the application of force to that body. Thus the law states that 'A body at rest tends to remain at rest and a body in motion tends to continue in the same consistent speed of motion in the same direction unless acted upon by an outside force'.

The law of acceleration

The second of Newton's laws refers to acceleration. The law states that 'The force required to accelerate a body is directly proportionate to the mass of the body, and to the acceleration produced, and in the same direction as the application of the force'.

It means that if a moving or propelling force applied to a body is doubled then the rate of acceleration will double. It also means that if a resisting force is applied in a direction directly opposite to the movement of the body, it will decelerate it. If it is a weak force it will stop the movement eventually. If it is equal in magnitude to the momentum of the object it will stop it quickly. If it is greater in magnitude than the momentum of the object it will reverse the direction of the object.

The law of reaction or counterforce

It is an intrinsic property of forces that they always act between two bodies rather than upon one body except when the force is applied upon a body freely suspended in space, when the action and the reaction will be between two different but connected parts of the same body. Another term used to describe reaction is counterforce; this may make the concept seem a little more simple to the student of mechanics.

Thus Newton stated 'To every action there is an equal and opposite reaction'. In the case of a person jumping from the ground the force supplied by the person jumping is insufficient to overcome the inertia of the earth, so the reaction of the earth is to push the person applying the force into the air.

Stored energy

The whole basis of the trampoline is the use of temporarily stored energy. The bed is mobile and is suspended upon elastics or springs attached to an outer frame approximately 105cm from the floor. The suspension system, when stretched, has the property of being able to spring back into its original position. The stretching stores the energy and the return to the original position releases that energy via the trampolinist. The amount of energy stored is dependent upon the momentum of the trampolinist and the elasticity of the suspension.

Thus any action that the trampolinist can produce which increases the depression of the bed and subsequently efficiently uses the stored energy will contribute to the efficiency of the jump, not only in height attained but, where necessary, the initiation of angular rotation by hip displacement. The actions which will contribute to the depression of the bed include body tension on impact, downward arms swing on impact, and extension of the legs and ankles after impact. Then a totally tense body extended as much as possible will use the release of the stored energy with as little loss of transfer as possible. At this point upward arm swing with some transfer of upward momentum will also help lift.

Where rotation is needed the hips can be displaced forwards or backwards dependent upon direction of rotation. Once again the performer must try to avoid loss of power by absorption in too slack a body or by over displacement causing loss of height. Too much lean may also cause a loss of efficiency.

The absorption of force

In contrast to the efficient use of stored energy, the absorption of force is necessary in order to stop. Having attained a great height for a routine the performer then has to stop in one or, at the maximum, two rebounds. There are penalties for lack of control on stopping and, with the enormous rebounding power of modern trampolines, the performer has to let the legs relax quickly without letting them collapse in order to come to rest under control. The spotter also has to be able to absorb some of the force of a performer who is falling on to, or over, the side of the trampoline. This can be risky for the performer and for the spotter who is there to hold the performer on or to slow the descent.

Kipping, one of the main skills of a competent coach, uses the principle of stored energy imparted by two people being directed to one person. The coach has to move fast enough as the rebound occurs to remove his weight (or at least most of it) from the bed. The performer will then be projected into the air with far greater force than possible with one manpower (*see* the section on kipping). If the coach absorbs the force, less lifting force is available for the performer.

Centrifugal force

Two performance demands come into the area of the effects of centrifugal force. One is the ability to tuck tightly in a somersault if necessary, the other is to 'kick out' from a tucked position to impress all watching. Centrifugal force also affects acceleration and deceleration.

The faster the somersault is after initiation of rotation the more centrifugal force there is, thus the harder it is to tuck tightly in the somersault. As soon as the tuck is tight the speed of rotation is increased dramatically and the body wants to open out. If this tendency to open out more, the faster the rotation, is used efficiently the 'kick out' will appear as if by magic. Many performers try to kick out from a very slow rotation and of course it looks forced. This is a very good illustration of the skilled performer and coach using the, not always obvious, mechanical principles, where the unskilled coach or performer looks for 'secrets' of performance. The whole skill then appears as a good open take-off with no more hip displacement than necessary, a rapid and tight tuck to give a fast increase in speed of rotation, ending with an early 'kick out' which decelerates the somersault for an easy landing under control.

Physics Terms

Force

That which changes a body's state of rest or uniform motion in a straight line. It can be a push or pull, it is measured in Newtons and given the symbol f.

Mass

The quantity of matter contained by a body. It is measured in kilograms and is given the symbol m.

Acceleration

The rate at which a body is speeding up or slowing down. It is measured in metres per second and given the symbol a.

According to Newton's second law of motion, these three quantities are related. The relationship is expressed as $f = m \times a$. Thus the larger the mass is, the more force you need to produce an acceleration.

Velocity

Speed in a specified direction. In common speech the terms 'speed' and 'velocity' are often used interchangeably and indistinguishably. In some situations the direction of motion is of no real concern, when it is convenient to use the term 'speed'. When direction and change of direction are important, the term 'velocity' should be used.

Weight

The force that a stationary body exerts on the ground. According to Newton's third law 'to every action there is an equal and opposite reaction'. Thus the ground exerts the same force upwards on the body. Weight is not the same as mass; for example, your weight on the moon is not the same as your weight on the earth, although your mass is the same.

Centre of mass

Sometimes called the 'centre of gravity'. The point at which the weight of a body appears to be acting. If you imagined the mass of a body all concentrated at a single point, that point would have to be the centre of mass.

Linear

Means in a straight line.

Angular

An adjective applied to rotation. There is an equivalent law to Newton's second law that relates to bodies which are rotating.

Angular velocity

The speed at which a body is rotating. In the absence of external influences, a body rotates about its centre of mass. Angular velocity is measured in radians per second and given the symbol ϑ (the Greek letter omega). One radian $= 57.3°$.

Torque

That which changes a body's state of rest or uniform angular velocity. It can either speed it up or slow it down. It is measured in Newton metres and given the symbol t. To get a torque you need two forces which are equal and opposite but not acting at the same point. The torque generated by these two forces is then equal to the product of one of the forces multiplied by their perpendicular distance apart.

Here torque is represented by $t = f \times d$.

Thus the bigger d is (d = perpendicular distance apart) the greater the torque resulting. For example a long-handled spanner exerts a greater torque when tightening a nut than a shorter-handled one.

Moment of inertia

If a body is large, i.e. it is not all concentrated at one point, then it requires work to be done on it to make it rotate. The amount of work depends upon the moment of inertia. It is measured in kilogram metres^2 and is given the symbol I. For a wheel of radius, r with all the mass concentrated on the circumference like a bicycle wheel, the moment of inertia is expressed as $I = Mr^2$. For a disc with the mass evenly distributed over the whole area, it works out that $I = \frac{1}{2}Mr^2$.

Angular acceleration

The rate at which angular velocity increases or decreases. It is measured in radians per second and given the symbol α (Greek letter alpha). The equivalent to Newton's second law is, torque = moment of inertia × angular acceleration. $T = I \times \alpha$. Thus the bigger the body the more torque you need to rotate it.

Linear momentum

This equals mass × linear velocity. It cannot change unless some external influence acts on the body.

Angular momentum

This equals moment of inertia × angular velocity. It cannot change unless some external influence acts upon the body.

Axis

In trampolining, the three axes normally referred to are:

[a] the longitudinal, from head to toe;

[b] the lateral, from side to side;

[c] the dorso–ventral, from back to front.

This presently corresponds to the normal somersaulting and twisting skills taught. There are, however, as many axes as there are applications of torque in the body. If you choose to apply a torque about a certain axis, then the angular acceleration is about that axis.

Radius of gyration

Imagine all the mass of the body to be concentrated at one point, but not at the centre of mass, and swinging about that point where the centre of mass used to be.

If the distance between this point and the old centre of mass is k (the radius of gyration), then the moment of inertia of the mythical arrangement is the same as the moment of inertia for the real body. In other words, the moment of inertia = Mk^2. For the bicycle wheel, k is the same as the actual radius. For the disc, $k = 0.707 \times$ actual radius. Thus a skater may be spinning with arms and legs outstretched. If he then brings his arms and legs together, the radius of gyration decreases. Hence the moment of inertia decreases and the rate of spinning increases (the product of $I \times \vartheta$ remains the same).

Examples of Twisting in Mid-Air

**From the piked position (*see* Figures
143a–d)**

**From the tucked position (*see* Figures
e–h)**

**From the pucked position (*see* Figures
i–l)**

Figure 143 shows that, in the starting positions, the longitudinal axes of the two major
segments of the body, the trunk and the legs,
are at, or near, right-angles to each other.
Thus rotation or twist about either axis is
met with resistance due to the moment of
inertia presented by the other body segment
and the angle of its longitudinal axis.

Normally the trunk is where the twist is
initiated. As the trunk and legs are brought
into line, and have a common axis, the rotation about the axis of the trunk is transferred
to that of the legs. The lines through the
trunk and legs showing the axes show the
relationships of the longitudinal axes.

Figure **143** Examples of twisting in mid-air

Action and reaction in flight (*see* Figure 144 below):

[a] tucking in flight;

[b] piking in flight;

[c] turning head and shoulders in flight;

[d] tipping the arms and head back in flight.

Decrease and increase of moment of inertia (*see* Figure 145 on opposite page).

Increase in speed of rotation (acceleration) of somersault in flight, by tucking. Deceleration by opening out to land.

[a] Longitudinal axis: head to toe and twisting move.

[b] Lateral axis: side to side forward and backward rotation.

[c] Dorso-ventral: (back to front) sideways rotation.

Rotation by Leaning

Eccentric force about the point of contact of the feet (at take-off). This can lead to over-rotation (*see* Figure 5).

Rotation by Displacement

More controlled on the spot from take-off to finish. No lean–no loss of height (*see* Figure 6).

Eccentric Force about the Longitudinal Axis

Sets up torque and rotation about the longitudinal axis. Arms out but no acceleration (*see* Figure 14).

Arms can be brought into the side to get acceleration (g). Setting up the twist (f).

Set up twist, arms out. Accelerate twist arms in, decelerate twist arms out again (*see* Figure 15).

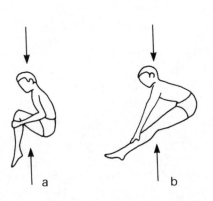

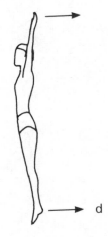

Figure **144** Action and reaction in flight

Eccentric Force about the Lateral Axis

Forward somersault.

Figure **145** Eccentric force about the lateral axis

Axes of rotation

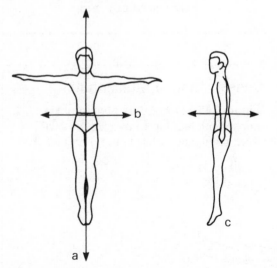

a Lateral axis – forward and backward somersault rotation

b Longitudinal axis – any twisting skill

c Dorso-ventral – side somersault, turntable

Figure **146**

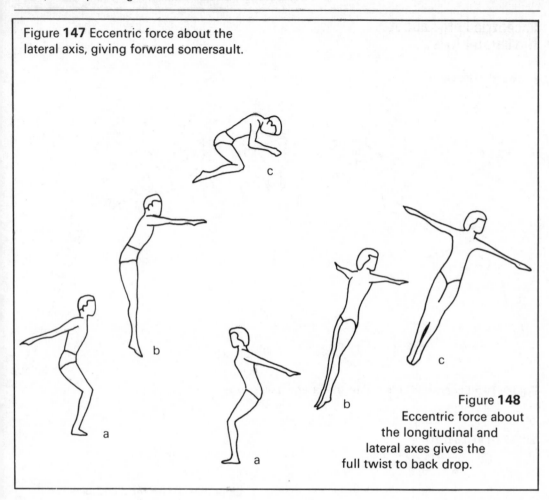

Figure **147** Eccentric force about the lateral axis, giving forward somersault.

Figure **148** Eccentric force about the longitudinal and lateral axes gives the full twist to back drop.

Conservation of Momentum

Figure **149** (a) Angular momentum is conserved, leading to over-rotation of front somersault after landing on feet (b).

Transfer of Angular Momentum

Figure **150** (a) Downward leg kick to give ball out; (b) downward kick to give back-ward cody rotation.

Relative Moment of Inertia Twisting Technique

One of the techniques used in trampolining is the one called RMI (relative moment of inertia) twisting. The twisting is initiated by moving one part of the body in the direction of twist whilst the body is in the tucked, piked or pucked shape, so that the moment of inertia of the part of the body which is not being twisted (which is at an angle to the twisted part) creates a resistance to the twist.

Examples of this can be seen in the illustrations of the fliffes, particularly the half in half out, the rudi out tucked and the piked rudi out. As the shoulders turn in the direction of twist they are resisted by the lower body, which is at an angle to the trunk. As the body is straightened out the twisting force (torque) is transferred to the whole of the body. Thus the angular momentum of the shoulders is transferred to the whole of the body, causing the whole body to twist. This technique is far easier to operate when the body is somersaulting, which leads to some questions. Is this because the gyroscopic effect of the rotating body gives an added resistance to the twist of the upper body, or is it because of the use of the sum total of momentum of the whole body to change the direction of one of the parts? A good explanation would be useful, although lack of one does not stop its effectiveness.

10

Trampoline Safety

'For safety, critical operations must be made easy and forgiving of mental aberration.'

In trampolining the performer can nowadays easily attain a height of 20–25 feet (6–8m), can land on the front or back of the body, can turn somersaults with or without twists, and in many movements sight of the bed is lost. Obviously there is a risk that some of these manoeuvres may go wrong and the performer may be injured.

Since there is a possibility of injury, safety is not only important: it is a legal obligation. All those who are involved in the teaching or organising of trampolining are legally obliged to take reasonable precautions to see that no person in their care is injured. Injury may occur because of human or mechanical failure. A mechanical failure may happen without warning. A hinge may snap because of metal fatigue, a spring may break or a leg brace become unwelded. Regular inspections of equipment by the user can help to avoid mechanical breakdown. Some human failure may also happen without warning. A knee may give way, a performer may lose concentration or be distracted, or there is an accident due to physical or psychological failure. Other human failure may be due to lack of knowledge, lack of foresight, lack of proper training, or lack of experience. Some of these failures may be legally blameworthy if proof of negligence can be established.

Legally blameworthy or not, there is much which can be done to avoid accidents. The sad part is that many accidents can lead to temporary or permanent damage to a pupil. All of us, both pupil and teacher, are human and likely at some time to make mistakes. It is important that the teaching and organising of trampolining are organised to reduce the risk of injury, and that teachers and pupils are actively taught about safety. Responsible behaviour should be expected and lack of it should be reprimanded.

Causes of Accidents

Accidents are usually caused by a failure at some stage in the sequential process which is undertaken during the course of teaching, learning or performance. Some understanding of the factors of human decision-making leading to performance may help both pupil and teacher to avoid wrong decisions and to recognise when danger lies ahead.

Decision-Making Process in Learning and Teaching

1 Input and sensation

Information comes via the senses, the eyes, the ears, the skin and the kinaesthetic system. This information has to be filtered for interpretation.

2 Perception

From the above input and sensation, certain information is filtered out by the brain, interpreted and passed on. If more than one item of information is coming in to the brain at once, only one can be acted upon at one time. The others are stored in the short-term memory, and may be recalled for action or discarded. Attention may be focused upon the most important, or the least important, message. This stage could be the first one in success or failure.

3 Decision

Whatever 'message' comes through, it requires a decision. This the pupil has to make in such a way that success is the result. The decision will be made either unaided, with the benefit of experience or with the help of instruction by the teacher. It will lead to an action, such as to duck in the crash dive or to tuck in the back somersault.

4 Action

The brain has sent the 'message' to the body for action and the ducking or tucking takes place.

All the above, highly complex processes have probably taken less than one second. During this very short passage of time, usually, we humans make the correct decisions or we take protective precautions to ensure safety if errors are made.

Figure 151 shows a diagrammatic representation of the information being received and translated and the sequence of decision and action.

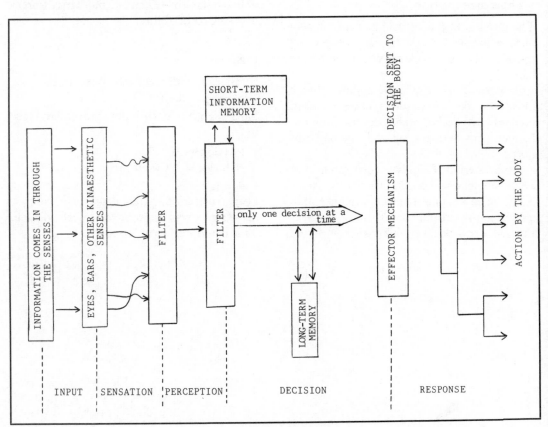

Figure **151** Receiving information and decision-making

Contributory Causes of Accidents

There are other problems which may arise during teaching that could lead to an accident. Some are listed below.

1 Visual illusion

The pupil is mistaken about what he thinks he sees. A common example of this is experienced at the railway station, when the train at the next platform starts to move and you feel that your train is moving. The pupil looks for visual cues and opens out from the somersault on seeing the white ceiling in mistake for the white bed.

2 False assumption

The pupil is in the rig and at take-off performs a double back; the teacher is expecting a single back. No check out was made before take-off.

Teacher and pupil both assume that a move will be started on a certain count. Neither has checked which count. This can happen with both the rig and manual support.

After a period of highly concentrated work a sudden loss of concentration can occur. The teacher assumes that the pupil is still in a good state of readiness instead of suggesting that a rest be taken. The teacher should have known from experience that fatigue induces loss of concentration.

3 Habit

Old habits die hard. They tend to re-appear when trying to correct skills. They can also appear under minor stress such as competition or training just before a competition.

4 Competitive instincts

Many performers are too highly competitive and drive themselves too far, too fast, trying to be the best. A pupil may attempt skills beyond his level of ability. The teacher may be even more competitive than the pupil and demand too much, trying to get success. Fear of loss of face by teacher or pupil may lead to over-taxing of ability.

5 Stress

Stress can be divided into three areas.

1 Environmental
Nose, lighting, flash bulbs, movement close by.

2 Physiological
Tiredness, sickness, injury.

3 Psychological
Fear, frustration, parental pressure, teacher pressure. Stress often impairs performance. This could lead to an accident.

11

Warm Up: General Principles for the Coach or Teacher

The Aim of 'Warm Up'

The aim of 'warm up' is to prepare the body physiologically for future exertion and thus to avoid strain, and possible injury to muscle and tendon, and even bone, from the very high exertion associated with athletic activity. Additionally, it is used to help prepare the performer psychologically for the physical tasks ahead. The following paragraphs should help the coach and the performer who wish to know a little more about this rather 'grey area' about which much is said but very little empirical evidence is available.

What Happens Physiologically

During exercise the muscles need extra oxygen and glycogen. The blood vessels dilate, the heart beat speeds up and the volume of blood pumped at each stroke increases, leading to a rise in blood pressure and a deeper and faster breathing pattern. Digestion slows down, glycogen in the liver becomes converted to glucose and is passed into the general circulation. The body heats up because of the increase in work and it is cooled by sweating and the evaporation of the sweat from the surface of the skin. In more simple terms the body adapts in a number of ways to enable more fuel to be better directed to the muscles. There is also general sympathetic nerve stimulation and the secretion of more

adrenalin than usual. The body heat increases by about 2°C.

Physiological Effectiveness of 'Warm Up'

Several studies have produced evidence that cooling of the muscles below normal temperature causes a loss of contractile time and excitability (*see* A. V. Hill, 'The Design of Muscles' *British Medical Bulletin*, 1956, vol. 12, ppo 165–6. 1956). De Vries, *Physiology of Exercise for P.E. and Athletics*, 1972 (second edition), reasoned that 'warm up' which results in increased temperature of the muscles and blood should improve the performance because:

[a] muscles would contract and relax faster;

[b] haemoglobin would give up more oxygen;

[c] muscles would contract with greater efficiency because of lower viscosity;

[d] metabolic processes would increase.

Jensen and Schultz, in a review (1977) of all the studies on 'warm up', found that the opinions of research were almost equally divided between the view that 'warm up' was beneficial and the view that it had no effect on performance. Not all the claims had been well researched, but it was most interesting that there was no evidence at all that 'warm up' had a negative effect.

The advocates of 'warm up' claimed that:

[a] it increased the rate and power of muscular contraction;

[b] related to a particular activity, it improved the necessary co-ordinations.

There is some evidence that muscles may be liable to tear because of lack of 'warm up'. The reasons given are that antagonistic muscles relax too slowly and incompletely and also that there may be a lack of synchronisation between neural impulses to specific muscle groups. Thus muscle groups which should be alternately contracting and relaxing, under the principle of reciprocal innervation, are contracting at the same time. Because of the great force being applied in opposite directions something must give, usually a muscle or a tendon.

To be most effective it seems that 'warm up' needs to be undertaken shortly before an event, not for so long or so strenuously that there is fatigue, and not so early that there is a cooling down. Between ten and thirty minutes seems to be the normal time spent 'warming up' by most athletes. Major games players spend very little time and racket players seem to be content with a knock up to get the eye in as well as warm up. Gymnasts and trampolinists seem to want to spend the most time on warming up. This may be because of the fear involved in these activities. Coaches showed little agreement about the length of time needed for 'warm up' or the optimum length of time between the end of warming up and the event.

Whatever the real physiological effects of 'warm up' may be, it seems that most coaches and performers do believe in its beneficial effects for better performance.

Psychological Effects of 'Warm Up'

During the run up to an event the performers and the coaches will normally be under some mental stress, the degree depending upon the type of personality of the participants. The physical activity of warming up will often help to relieve this stress by reassuring the performer that all systems are working, and that his skills have not suddenly been lost. Often one sees gymnasts, trampolinists or divers mentally reassuring themselves just before going on the apparatus by acting out the sequence of their performance. They wish to check that they know what to do even though they have performed hundreds of times. They do not wish to suffer from loss of sequence memory for a routine or single complicated move. This can be well illustrated by the few lines of verse below.

A centipede was happy quite until a frog
  in fun
Said 'Pray which leg comes after which?'
This set his mind in such a pitch
He lay distracted in a ditch
Figuring how to run.

Psychologically the athlete must be allowed to feel happy about the time before the event. Many and varied will be the activities to reduce the pre-competition stress. Trampolining has an official warm up time. After many different arrangements over the years, one of the best does seem to be the provision of a general warm up period for some time before the event in which all can indulge their particular warm up or pre-competition rituals, followed by a thirty second practice on the competition trampoline just before the event. This is done in groups of the six who are next to compete. Although the time scale is short, the physiological effects are still advantageous. The rules of trampolining have laid down that 'warm up' trampolines identical to those used in the competition must be available.

12

Sports Injury

All sport, where the body is moved quickly in space or projectiles are thrown or batted, may be injurious for the participants or spectators. Some injuries are caused by the impact of the projectiles and some by the body itself being the projectile. In addition, there are injuries caused by internal stress or strain. Sport, by its very nature, imposes stress and strain on the mechanical parts of the body being used. This can cause instant injury or a gradual decline in the painless and efficient use of an affected part of the body.

Impact Injuries

Injuries caused by the impact of articles used in sport may be quite severe. Being impaled on a javelin or dented by a cricket ball or bruised, or worse, by impact with the trampoline frame or breaking the neck by impact of the body on the bed are usually the most severe of sporting injuries.

Leverage or Strain Injuries

The injuries caused by mechanical forces generated inside the body include strains, stress fractures, ruptures and such painful conditions as 'tennis elbow' (bursitis) or pulled tendons. They are usually caused by the stress of trying extra hard to make a movement whilst the body is too tense, off-balance or unfit. These injuries are quite common and may not cause too much of a problem to the athlete at first but if not treated they may develop into more serious disorders. Occasionally tendons may rupture or bones may actually break under the stress of intense effort or whilst working with the body in an unusual position.

Overload Injuries

There is another form of injury which may develop through the continuous placing of a part of the body under heavy training loads during the years of development of a young person, or in preparation for a competition by any athlete. Enthusiasm may overcome good sense even with the best of intentions. The fact that there is no obvious problem may lead teachers and parents to think that there is no danger. Training should be carried out carefully, injuries should be allowed to heal before heavy training is resumed, and any persistent recurrence of the same injury should lead the responsible teacher or parent to consult with either their own doctor or, preferably, one with an interest in or qualification in sports medicine.

Factors Influencing Injury in Sport

A number of factors affecting the acquisition of skill were mentioned in the section on skill learning. In the same way there are some factors which affect an individual's vulnerability to certain types of injury. Some of these factors are the same as those which affect skill learning, they act in a different way. The factors are: age, environment, fitness, physique, physiological fitness, sex, technique, plus, in the past ten years, drugs to improve performance. Each factor has to be taken into account throughout an athlete's career and sensible decisions have to be taken from time to time in the light of developments.

The sport of trampolining can give rise to injury to the back, knees, shoulders and ankles, in particular. There is also a danger to the neck from failure to complete back and front somersaults successfully. The commonest type of injury seems to be muscle strain, twisting of the joints and compressions injuries rather than those resulting from hard contact with solid objects.

Age of Participants

In every activity age plays an important part. It is possible for the trampolinist to continue well into middle age, although care should be taken to avoid the highly complicated skills, failure in which could mean possible serious injury. Injury can occur at any age. However in the pre-adolescent years, long-term functional disability may result from muscle or tendon injuries caused by overwork and exertion before the pupil is physically ready to handle the heavy demands of competition.

At present competition is undertaken by performers at all ages from under nine to over eighteen. The young do take part in senior competitions and many champions in the senior categories are still in their teens. At international level the standard of training is high and the risks of injury increase. The lower age limit for taking part in senior international competition is twelve, but some parents and coaches have fought to have it lowered so that their pupils may be eligible. They do not apparently consider that there is any danger or, if they do, they are not letting it interfere with their ambition.

13

Basic First Aid and Emergency Procedures

THESE NOTES ARE ONLY A GUIDE.
WHEREVER POSSIBLE QUICKLY OBTAIN
PROFESSIONAL HELP OR ADVICE.

In all sport where bodies are moving about quickly along the ground or through the air, there is a likelihood of some injury.

If there is injury, action will be needed. It may not be possible to get professional help at once and in some cases of very minor injury it may not be needed. For the safety of the injured person, and to protect yourself from possible litigation, make sure that you are a help not a disaster to the injured party.

These notes, compiled by Stephen McDonald to give guidance on basic emergency procedures, are simple and should be studied and remembered, or better still copied out and kept in the club locker for reference. At the very least they will help you not to make a mistake in the case of serious injury. Dr McDonald is a trampoline coach and Secretary to the Technical Committee of the British Trampoline Federation. The injuries listed are related to actual trampoline situations and as such will be recognised by coaches. They are classified as minor, more serious and very serious.

Minor Problems

Table 1

	Injury	Cause and Recognition	Procedure
1	**Cuts, Grazes**	Sliding landing on unprotected areas usually knees and elbows. Minor bleeding.	Clean with soap and water, blot dry and leave grazes open to dry, use plaster or a dry dressing to cover cuts. Gaping cuts should go to hospital.
2	**Bruises**	Usually a direct blow from another part of the body or by hitting the frame. Immediate swelling–does not change colour immediately	Cool either with water or a suitable cooling spray. Avoid wintergreen or similar sprays. Elevate the part to reduce discomfort.

| 3 **Bitten Tongue** | Common when chin is hit either by a knee in tucked shapes or on landing. Bleeds very heavily. | Usually stops very rapidly on its own. If not, pinch the tongue with clean finger and thumb over the bleeding area on upper and lower surfaces. |
| 4 **Nose Bleed** | Usually a bang on the nose. May bleed heavily. | Keep the head upright and pinch the nose between finger and thumb at the junction between the hard (upper) and soft parts. Apply pressure for **five minutes**. |

More Serious Problems
Table 2

1 **Ankle Injuries**	Usually the ankle is injured in twisting landings. Impossible to assess bony damage without X-rays.	Keep cool or spray as above. Elevate to limit discomfort. Wise not to bandage and to get part X-rayed. Do not let patient walk on it.
2 **Knee Injuries**	Twisting landings can damage the cartilages. Intense pain in the knee joint itself. Knee held slightly bent. Landing with the weight well back on a straight leg may cause over straightening.	Support the knee with a pad behind the knee so that it remains slightly bent. Do not allow weight-bearing. Needs professional advice.
3 **Wrist and Forearm**	Landing on out-stretched arm. Look for deformity.	As bones may be broken, **must** be X-rayed. Put arm in a sling to support weight. Check collar bone as well.

Very Serious Injuries
Table 3

| 1 **Head Injury** | Hitting head on frame or spotter or on falling off. May be dazed or unconscious. | **Must go to hospital**. Before movement check no possible damage to neck. Best to get **trained** help immediately and warn them the neck may be injured. If unconscious, turn on to side. |

| 2 | **Spinal Injury** | Landing on head or high on back or neck with body weight folding neck forwards. | **Make no attempt to move the patient. Do not climb on to the bed – movement may cause further damage. Get ambulance personnel and warn them of spinal injury. First aid training does not qualify you to deal with this type of injury.** If possible, get some firm base under the bed to allow the patient to be moved without the springs bouncing him about. |
| 3 | **Broken Limb Bone** | Any awkward landing. Usually the deformity is obvious. | For a leg, use the other leg as a splint by lightly bandaging together with pads between ankle and knee. For an arm, use a sling and keep supported and immobile. |

14

The Learning and Teaching of Skill

According to Knapp, skill is the 'learned ability to bring about pre-determined results with the maximum certainty, often with the minimum of effort'.

The implications of the above succinct statement are wide and far-reaching, both for teacher and pupil. Learning and training are very complicated areas whose results cannot be predicted with certainty. Each pupil and each teacher is different. There are only guide-lines for us to follow. These do give help to those involved in both learning and teaching, but much remains to be done in this area.

An attempt will be made in the following pages to set out some of the common factors in skill learning and teaching, so that the reader may be able to use the information set out in what is hoped to be a logical order.

As many areas as possible will be covered in brief so that the potential teacher will be able to devise for later use a programme of work for any pupil. The programme will not be set out specifically in these pages but sufficient information will be included for most needs in clubs and schools.

Personal Factors of the Pupil

These are inherited and cannot be altered. Some coaches go as far as to run selective tests to eliminate those who do not come into certain categories of height, weight or slimness, in the attempt to make more sure of success in the quest for competition winning. However, there are so many factors which are built into excellence that the computation of them all into a readily recognisable pattern is impossible. Nevertheless, it can be said that for certain activities some physical characteristics will make a high level of success unlikely. A five foot tall high jumper is not likely to figure in world ratings.

Age

Age is a major consideration in determining the level of achievement of a pupil. Although there is nothing to stop a very young child taking part in trampolining, learning high level skills may be too difficult. There is much controversy about the age at which children should start on the advanced and complex moves. Certainly children of seven and nine are capable of very difficult and complex skills both on the trampoline and in gymnastics—generally those moves which need momentum rather than sheer strength. It has been found quite often that the younger performers, who at first have a great motor ability, seem, as they change size and proportion and mature mentally, to lose interest, or lose something which makes them unable to fulfil their earlier promise. There can be a very high level of stress in the form of fear or pressure to succeed from coach or parent which causes the young performer to avoid further progress in the sport.

Perhaps the parent or coach may fail to provide the same motivation which spurred on the pupil at an earlier stage, or perhaps the developing personality of the child may cause a change of attitude. Maybe some research in this area, now that there is more opportunity to make contact with those who are young and able, would help to solve some of the problems encountered by coach and pupil alike.

It is obvious that younger pupils with exceptional ability may be given many hours of tuition and may be afforded more attention and perks than older pupils of similar talent or achievement. It would be as well to try to make sure that young pupils are protected from the bad effects of too much pressure to advance to high levels of skill too soon.

There does not seem to be any optimum age to start trampolining, but ten or eleven is not too late. To reach the top it would seem that there is a need to start by about the age of ten. Many champions are teenagers, especially amongst the girls. Trampolining is an activity which can be enjoyed into middle age. Of course it is suggested that the more difficult, and possibly dangerous skills are not attempted by the older novice. Reaction times will have slowed and the build-up work may prove too difficult. However, most of us do realise our limitations and are only too ready to swap heady excitement for aesthetic simplicity, which can be exciting enough if performed at moderate height.

Sex

It seems that physical sex differences in children up to the age of eleven are of little consequence. At adolescence there are marked differences which appear in the physical structure. Performance tends to be similar but girls do, at the moment, peak at a lower performance level than boys. This may be purely because they have less power, which is needed for the most advanced skills, rather than any differences in learning characteristics. The girls certainly do not lack in the courage necessary for many of the skills. It is evident that more information is needed in this area, and there is some evidence that girls are beginning to advance into areas of physical achievement previously thought beyond them. Very little information is documented.

Intelligence

There does seem to be some correlation between intelligence and learning. Many arguments have been put forward on this subject, especially by those who assume that they are intelligent. On balance it would seem that the intelligent person has an advantage when it comes to learning complex skills which need some degree of understanding before approaching the practical performance of them. However, there seems to be little correlation between intelligence and learning for simple skills.

Whatever research is being carried out into the problems of learning it is difficult to structure suitable tests which fairly and accurately measure the previous experience or the intelligence of the pupil. Very little empirical evidence is available.

Individual Differences

The innate individual differences can be classified as structural, functional, organismic and perceptual. The general word to describe these sectors of the body is 'morphology'. These natural characteristics gradually change as life progresses from childhood to old age. They consist of such elements as height, weight, length of limb, size of trunk, acuity of vision, ability to receive and interpret information, speed of response, etc. They are interrelated and interdependent and are the main contributory factors to the unique movement patterns of each person and the individual capacity to learn skills.

Structural

Concerning the design and structure of the skeletal and muscular system.

Functional

Concerning the movements physically possible using the skeletal and muscular system.

Organismal

Concerning size, weight, limb length, age, and sex, all of which have some important restrictions or advantages when any person is involved in skill learning. They have an important effect upon the total skill learning capabilities of the individual.

Perceptual

Concerning the reception of information by the body, the processing and the ultimate response in carrying out certain goal-directed movements within a defined time-scale.

Psychological

In addition to all the above factors, there are certain psychological effects brought about by fear, stress or other emotions, which may have marked effects upon performers. One has often heard of the gifted performer who is not a very good competitor and the less talented one who makes it by guts against apparently superior opponents. This again is an area where prediction of effects and behaviour is not easy. The ability to deal with the problem is one of the attributes which distinguishes the good coach from the ordinary coach.

Environmental Factors

The above factors are to do with innate abilities that cannot be changed. Other fixed factors are the types of equipment used, the surroundings, the rules and any aesthetic or technique standards in operation at the time of learning. They too must be conformed

with and present challenges to the ability of the pupil and the coach.

Mechanical

Overcoming the problems of gravity, mass and inertia can be seen as sub-goals of the main task in the learning of motor skills. The ability to deal with those problems will have a marked effect upon success or failure in learning any motor skill. Certain mechanical principles will apply to the actions needed to produce purposeful movement (*see* section on mechanics). The principles are unalterable and apply constantly. They are fairly easy to understand but the practical application of them in a learning or problem-solving situation may prove far more difficult. It is, however, important that the teacher or coach has a very clear knowledge of the principles to facilitate description and analysis of movement tasks and to give a good basis for quantitive and qualititive analysis.

In addition to the factors mentioned above, it is necessary to consider one other important idea. The summation of internal forces is a concept which can be described as the utilisation of generated muscular force in the most efficient way possible to carry out the motor tasks in which we are involved. In many cases this generated muscular force is not applied in the best way, resulting in much wasted effort, poor performance and poor quality skill.

The Ergonomic Cycle

The whole process of skill can also be classified as an ergonomic cycle which is broken down into successive operative sections or phases. For most actions the ergonomic cycle can be broken down into three simple sections: the preparation section, the main/ major action section and the repositioning, or resetting section. This breakdown suits gymnastic and trampoline skills admirably.

Phased skilled movements are the general pattern for gymnastics and trampolining and the above sections will suit the phasing roughly corresponding with 'take-off', 'flight' and 'landing' or 'landing with preparation for the next take-off'.

The first stage in the cycle of the phased movement on the trampoline is one of preparation of the body for the take-off. This takes place as the body descends to the bed, and continues as the body sinks into the bed and as it rises from the bottom level of the depression of the bed. The body is moved into the shape suitable for the production of forward or backward rotation, twisting, rotating, and twisting or rotating from the front or back landing position. Each of the above variations needs a slightly different position of readiness from each of the others from which the particular take-off is made. The next stage will be the main/major action stage during which the body is moved from the preparatory stage via the appropriate movements of the limbs into the main part of the whole skill. This involves power, direction and sensitivity of movement starting from the main trunk and continuing the chain of movement successively through to the smaller muscles operating the ends of the limbs. These successive actions can be used to generate more power, more speed, more accuracy or sensitivity of movement because of the increased time-scale in which the movement is being developed. The repositioning or resetting phase or section is the one in which the body is returned to the position of readiness for the next movement, for coming to a controlled stop, or for carrying out a change of direction.

The above constraints do not have any readily visible demarcation lines but flow easily from one stage to the next as successive stages of skilled movement. The teacher will need to be able to see the general outline of each stage so that proper analysis of each section may be carried out. Each successive stage is dependent upon the success of the previous stage for its own success. An incorrect starting phase may make it impossible to carry out the task in the required way to the desired end. So much adjustment, and so much time for the adjustment, will be needed that the rest of the timing, so important a factor in skilled movement, will be out of phase. Thus it may be that the preparatory phase is normally the most important in the cycle, if more or less importance can be attached to any phase.

If the concept of the summation of internal forces is accepted, the following pattern can be seen. The body is put into an advantageous position to use the stretch reflex. This helps to generate more contractile power over the greatest usable distance possible. The limbs can then be brought into action successively over a greater distance, applying power for longer and giving the possibility of better goal-directed application, since the force exerted by a muscle or a group of muscles is directly proportional to muscle length. The summation process of transferring the force to each successive segment of the body involved in the action can be likened to a whiplash effect for the generation of maximum speed of movement. The crack at the end of the movement of the whip is generally supposed to be the cord or thong travelling so fast that it passes through the sound barrier.

All the above personal and mechanical factors will affect the learner. All the morphological factors are interrelated and interdependent. They are the main contributory factors to the individual movement patterns of each person's learning skills. The teacher or coach will be involved in trying fo fit each person to the closed skills and the environment in the best possible way. It is the influence of the above factors which gives uniqueness to each pupil, which may be an advantage or the opposite.

Skill Learning and Other Factors Affecting the Acquisition of Skill

The learning of any skill is a very complicated process. In addition to the personal, mechanical and environmental factors involved, there is a number of important areas which come under the classification of 'factors affecting the acquisition of skill' and consist of those areas of knowledge about the learning of skills which seem to change from time to time as more information and results of research become available. These factors can help to change the pupil in a developmental way, with regard to the learning of skill. If the principles are followed it should be possible to help the pupil to learn more easily than by a system of random trial and error.

The Role of the Teacher

The role of the teacher or coach is to observe and analyse and to supply the right kind of information to the pupil at the right time. In order to be able to do this the teacher needs to know a great deal about the task being carried out. This should come from a very careful analysis of each skill, carried out in an objective way. It is not always necessary for the teacher to become proficient in all skills being taught. He must find out what factors affect the learning of the skill and how best to arrange their presentation in a variety of ways to suit best the individual learners. He must be clear about what is to be taught, and the pupil about what is to be learned. It helps if this can be made clear and precise and also if clear information is given on skills which cover several aspects of a function or which may require some flexibility or performance. Practically the teacher will need to apply principles which are appropriate to the problem and to measure their effectiveness.

The teacher will need to evaluate the effectiveness of any scheme of training being used. Adjustments will be needed. It will be better if they are made one at a time so that the effect may be more easily measured against previous performance. Many things must be considered with regard to the training programme, and amongst them is the type of information and how it is put out to the pupil. Listed below are some of the forms of information which can be given to the pupil.

> *Perceptual cues*
> *Visual aids*
> *Diagrams*
> *Graphics*
> *Knowledge of results*

It is necessary to regulate the supply of all these forms of information to the pupil to avoid overloading, which has a negative effect, or underloading which wastes the time of both teacher and pupil. As the pupil develops there is a change in information-absorbing capacity. Small amounts of verbal information should be given well spaced out in each session to give plenty of time for assimilation and learning. If demonstrations are used it is important to draw attention to perceptual cues. In the case of skills where phasing or difficult timing is needed, advance cues must be highlighted. These timing cues may be verbal, e.g. calling 'tuck' or 'stretch', or visual such as 'when you see the bed'. There are other cues; 'wait till you are half-way round and then...'; 'hold on longer than you think is necessary'; 'you need to feel that you are floating upward': they are all useful at times.

The teacher may use supports or physical guidance combined with suitable progressions. The support must not be restrictive and must be compatible with the skill to be learned, or the pupil may learn incorrectly or place too much reliance on the support. It is also important that the teacher has some alternative methods of support to suit different pupils and ensure maximum progress (*see* chapter on support methods). Manual or mechanical support will be especially useful if the trampoline skills are dangerous.

The teacher will have to plan the programme for the pupil so that, as far as possible, the training proceeds towards the desired objective with good demonstrations, good quality instruction and accurate analysis of the movements to be performed. Use may be made of film and video, wherever possible, to show the errors or good points of performance. Verbal direction is very useful in the early stages: it should be brief and directed towards better observation by the pupil. Later verbal instruction can help to make analysis more meaningful to the pupil.

When involved in analysis, the teacher will need to check observations against objective tests, to beware of prejudice and defiencies in observational powers and to work constantly towards more specific knowledge of the movements being taught. If dealing with competitors the teacher must be available to give information on the visual effect of the pupil's performance on the judges and to keep working on the correction of fundamental errors with a view to improving overall performance.

Factors to be Taken into Account by the Teacher

The role of the teacher is most important when one comes to the organisation and content of the programme. The skills on the trampoline are of the 'closed' variety, that is they conform to decided paterns of movement, have certain fashionable ways of performance, are put into routines and are measured against commonly accepted norms.

It would seem that the 'closed' skills of the trampoline can be better learned by spending a great deal of time on the formation of good habits and the development of

conditioned responses. Thus the teacher has to ensure that the learner works on the good habits and responses and gets the feelings of pleasure associated with success in the performance of these 'good' habits.

Motivation

There will be problems. There will be periods of despair and loss of sense of progress, and the problem of changing habits which are incorrect but give satisfaction. In all the problem areas it is the teacher's job to try to keep the pupil motivated. Failure will lead to loss of motivation. The teacher must, by careful assessment of progress, systematic guidance in the right direction and analysis of problems, try to avoid loss of motivation due to lack of success.

Success is one of the key factors in motivation. Other important factors are:

fun must be present in all learning;

children need fun more than adults–but both need it;

success and praise honestly won and given will help;

unpleasant situations do not help learning;

success in well-designed proficiency tests may help increase development especially of fundamentals;

competition used carefully improves performance;

competition with careful preparation of good performance may lead to avoidance of failure–not success;

continual failure in competition does not usually lead to success.

At all times only work at a level which the pupil can handle successfully. This may indicate a need for intelligent subdivision of the task. The subdivisions must not change the task intrinsically but must make small successes helpful in advancing the development of the total skill. There is a problem when the pupil loses a skill and tries by determination to get it back, instead of going over some of the progressions in order to try to rediscover the complete skill by following the same pattern used in the original learning.

Learning Curves

Physical skills cannot be learned without 'having a go'. Different people will need different numbers of trials to achieve success. Total progress is usually measured in some way; this can be by means of a graph and is shown as a performance curve. It can be easily seen from the curve that there are periods of no measurable learning (this does not necessarily mean that nothing is happening) and periods of accelerated learning. The periods of no measurable learning are sometimes called plateaux. It can be very discouraging to stay on a plateau, and this can happen for a number of reasons. The teacher should try to avoid as much as possible the effects upon the pupil of remaining on a plateau. Use encouragement, helpful technical advice, a change of routine or a short rest from routine. Working on good form from the very beginning will give a sound basis for future development, as opposed to a method which limits development although apparently faster at a specific stage of learning. Good instruction from an expert at the beginning will usually be the best course of action.

Knowledge of Results and Principles

The pupil will benefit from the knowledge of the results of his actions. Improvement in performance is unlikely without this knowledge, which acts as a guide to the learner. The learner should be given knowledge which is as exact as possible to help select the good elements in performance as soon as possible after completion, to try to improve future performance. Practical experiments in skill learning seem to bear this out. Knowledge of skill learning principles is essential for the teacher, so that a constant check can be made on the informaiton being given and a ready made reference system is available at all times. For the pupil it may not be essential but it would not seem to be negative in effect. For the more intelligent pupil it could prove to be a considerable aid to progress, permitting self checking during practice periods.

Practice

Practice is important and does use a large part of the working time of the pupil. However, there does seem to be some distinction between practice and training. Practice according to some authorities, consists of repetition of skills or parts of skills. Training is different because it consists of repetition with guidance and information by the teacher and should lead hopefully to further learning or progress. Practice may not lead to progress and change but may just be designed to keep physical skills 'grooved'. It is part of the training programme and is not always so closely directed by the teacher as the training or developmental section.

Distribution of Practice

Practice should be little and often at first, and can be for longer periods as acclimatisation takes place. Children and beginners can stand only short periods, and experienced adults can stand longer periods with benefit. Practice should be intense, of good quality and meaningful, and should stop as soon as bad habits begin to appear or there will be too much tension giving bad performance and indicating stress.

Massed Practice

Massed practice or frequent practice sessions can be used when the skill is of low level or does not require too much energy or a very high level of concentration. Beginners may therefore benefit from this type of practice if it is possible to organise.

Spaced Practice

Spaced practice has greater intervals of time between sessions. It may be more necessary when the skill level is higher, if it is complicated or dangerous. Practice of fliffus moves may involve so much concentration in the learning stage that only two or three attempts per training session may be possible before the pupil has had enough. This may be due to psychological as well as physical fatigue. As the fliffus becomes a relatively simple move to the pupil, he may be able to handle many more repetitions per session or to have more practice sessions.

Pressure Practice

This type of practice, where the performer has to carry out many repetitions in a short space of time, is much more used in ball games where a single skill can be carried out at very frequent intervals by pupils or a machine is used to pass the ball to a single pupil for a particular skill practice. The interval between passes can thus be varied from slow to very fast. On the trampoline repetition of the same skill in swingtime may be seen as a pressure practice. Some skills at elementary and intermediate level can be grooved in this way. The pressure may be used to try to sharpen up the thought sequences and responses and also to avoid the waste of time taken by three or four jumps before each skill.

Mental or Verbal Practice

Mental practice, thinking about a move, or verbal practice, talking through it, does seem to have some benefit and many top performers are seen indulging in it. It does seem to be beneficial to the more experienced performers since they have complete and accurate mental images of the skill. The less experienced performer has only partly formed images which are still in the process of constant and possibly considerable change. It is not as good as, nor will it replace, physical practice but it may help in periods when physical practice is not possible. It may also help the pupil to concentrate on the move before physical practice. It may be one of the factors in the situation where a pupil improves even when no actual physical practice has taken place for some space of time.

The Subdivision of Skills

There has been much discussion amongst physical educationalists about the best methods of teaching the skills of sport. The problem is that there are so many variable factors affecting both the teacher and the learner that it is difficult to find enough evidence from research to indicate any particular course of action. In trampolining and gymnastics, progressions have traditionally been used for most of the skills being taught, often combined with manual or mechanical support. The support is given because psychologically the pupil cannot cope with the new and strange kinaesthetic sensations being registered whilst moving through the air, and panic may cause him to freeze. The freeze stops all thought processes and actions, although the momentum already established still has its effect. Thus it may be seen that the fear and tension present when an unprepared pupil first attempts a complicated skill may prevent him from approaching it with the confidence necessary for success. Failure could be physically disastrous, and the teacher or coach should not risk this result lightly.

Transfer of Training

This is an area of controversy. There is conflicting evidence that the learning of new skills is affected positively, negatively, or not at all. However, it is useful to note the different types of transfer.

Positive Transfer

When previous training aids the learning of a new skill, there is said to be positive transfer. Thus, the person who can ice-skate should find it easier to learn to roller skate. The skills are similar although not the same, and the previous knowledge should help.

Negative Transfer

When previous learning makes a task more difficult to learn then transfer is said to be negative. Thus the badminton player may have more problems in learning tennis than the completely new pupil.

Interference

In trampolining the problem most frequently met is that of interference. The person who has just learned the double twisting back somersault may have considerable difficulty in performing the full or single twisting back somersault. However, the problem can be overcome in time, and the performance of the double twisting back then makes the performance of the single twist easier. Some skills with a similar start but a different ending can also be said to be causing interference in performance. This can often be a considerable problem in the performance of competitive routines. This interference tends to appear under stress, when there is often a reversion to the old or previously learned skill. Competition can produce stress in many performers and then there is sometimes a manifestation of interference.

Transfer, it can be said, is not automatic or predictable and in the main does depend on the ability of the individual. The physical educationalists have a tendency to assume that there is often a large amount of positive transfer and act accordingly without checking further. The teacher must always try to find evidence, or at least run a personal objective check out.

Retention of Skill

The important question to be asked about retention of skill is: how long can a person retain a skill with no or very little practice, and how much practice is necessary to establish a skill at an automated stage which favours long term retention?

It seems that well-learned motor skills are retained, to a high degree, over a number of years even with little or no practice. Examples of this are cycle riding, skating, swimming, playing the piano and typing. If the basic fundamentals have been well learned, they are usually retained and can be repolished in a short time. A gap in the performance of the activity does not necessarily mean that there will be an unrecoverable loss of skill.

Permanent retention of the skill is best achieved by overlearning and frequent review of the skill. This is also true of bad habits which indicates that, at all times, the pupil should be schooled in good habits from the start. This might seem obvious, but so often is ignored by the teacher or coach either through ignorance or poor application of principles.

The Analysis of Skill

Most untutored or self-tutored learning proceeds by trial and error. It may be a long time before errors are discovered, perhaps too late to avoid the formation of bad habits. Any teacher or coach should be able to analyse the skills to be taught and, to a large extent, eliminate trial and error as the only source of problem information or problem solving. A pupil normally wants to know of progress in skill learning (knowledge of results); self analysis should help in the process of learning new skills or improving those already held. It is far better if the teacher has plenty of experience in problem solving. Analysis usually plays an important part in this process and the teacher should play a central role. There are four main areas of analysis.

[a] The analysis and understanding of performance in order to give related feedback, appropriate to the skill being learned.

[b] The analysis and understanding of a particular skill.

[c] The analysis and evaluation of individual performance.

[d] Self analysis and evaluation of movement.

It is necessary to be able to distinguish between the analysis of skill and the analysis of performance. The analysis of skill is descriptive of the skill itself, whilst the analysis of performance is related to the manner in which the particular pupil carries out the skill to be learned.

A systematic approach to analysis will help all involved to find out:

[a] what is being looked at;

[b] what is being looked for;

[c] how to produce systematically whatever change is needed in what is learned already, or is being learned.

The ability to observe and to analyse is valuable to the teacher or coach for the following reasons.

[a] Attention is focused on the sequence of events.

[b] The most significant aspects of a particular skill can be identified and the attention of the pupil may be drawn to them.

[c] It systematises thinking about the relationship between the movement and the outcome.

[d] It picks out the identifiable elements of the movement, to use them during instruction as feedback.

[e] It aids in the evaluation of the development of a particular skill, and the assessment of performance over a period of time.

In order to help the teacher or coach in his analysis of movement, it is suggested that a systematic approach be made and the following areas be covered.

[a] The goal of the movement.

[b] The critical features involved in the movement.

[c] The single aspect of the skill clearest in the mind. The key to the movement.

[d] Any unnecessary movements which make the skill more difficult.

[e] Critical features executed or not executed.

[f] The degree of goal achievement.

[g] The evaluation of efficiency.

[h] Feedback, from coach to pupil and pupil to coach.

From all the preceding sections, it can be seen that the role of the teacher or coach is of paramount importance. This role is such that generally there would be very little progress if all learning was carried out unaided and all pupils were left to proceed by trial and error. The knowledge and experience of the teacher, accumulated over a long period of time, can help avoid many pitfalls and problems for the pupil. The teacher must also realise that there is no way to acquire experience as a teacher, other than taking part in the act of teaching. The information contained in this section should be of help, if used as a reference system. All good teachers will realise that they use many of the ideas almost without knowing that they are working systematically towards achievable goals. Maybe they will be able to become a little more organised and to eliminate some of their own learning problems. The following list of qualities of a coach will help the inexperienced and the experienced teacher or coach to identify their own. Note the negative ones.

Positive Qualities of the Coach

(Assessed from the study of many college coaches.)

[a] Orderly–organised–looking ahead.

[b] Outgoing–warm towards people.

[c] Has a developed conscience.

[d] Able to handle emotions under stress.

[e] Open, trusting–not defensive.

[f] Natural leader.

[g] Able to accept responsibility.

[h] High level of tenacity.

[i] Emotionally mature–prepared to face reality.

[j] Able to express freely his natural aggressiveness.

Many coaches also display the following traits.

[a] Not interested in dependency needs or able to display emotional support.

[b] Tend to be conservative with respect to new learning or ideas–not prepared even to try to use them.

The coach should try to develop the following.

[a] A realisation that every pupil is unique.

[b] Recognition of the characteristics which distinguish the good from the poor competitor.

[c] A study of psychological needs to try to improve performance.

[d] A positive relationship with regard to behaviour traits of pupils.

[e] A check system for his own psychological blind spots.

[f] Modification of own negative attitudes by bringing them out into the open.

[g] Honesty.

[h] Psychological insight.

The Role of the Pupil

Although many words have been used describing the qualities of the pupil, the programme for the pupil and the improvement of the pupil, it is important to realise that, without the pupil, none of us would be in the business of teaching, coaching, instructing, or writing books of instruction.

The pupil is the one who has to learn. He is the one who has to suffer the defeats and setbacks, and, possibly, the injuries both physical and mental, at the hands of the teacher, coach or instructor. Often it is the pupil who gets the blame for failure and has very little say in the matter, especially if young.

The pupil should be able to express feelings about the activity and the demands of the teacher. This may be difficult, for the young pupil, but still has value. He should be honest when communicating with the teacher, especially when concerned about a problem area. Recognition of a problem by a pupil is a step in the right direction and helps to get nearer to the solution. So often, the teacher expects the pupil to act like a robot and so often, the pupil is content to do just that. The pupil should stop and question when unsure and be prepared to trust when experience of the teacher has enabled a trust to be built. He should recognise that the teacher is not infallible, but is putting a lot of time and effort into the development of the pupil. Co-operation and discussion over tasks set should help more speedy progress. The pupil should not expect to progress too fast, but should realise that it takes time to learn and that it may be necessary to go back a little way and start again. He should try to be as knowledgeable as possible about the programme of work, be prepared to work without the undivided attention of the teacher and develop an attitude towards other pupils which will engender mutual help in the group.

The Effects of Stress on the Learning of Skill and the Performance of the Pupil

One of the major factors affecting the acquisition and performance of skilled movements is stress. Stress is real and concrete but it is non-specific and can be caused by almost any agent. It can give benefit and cause suffering. It affects soldiers in war, mothers caring for children, parachutists, test pilots, all those who take part in potentially dangerous activities, businessmen and those who are ambitious or wish to progress. Into a number of the above activities comes the athlete, especially the trampolinist, and therefore the coach.

Several general factors have been outlined from the many works on stress. These are:

[a] the greater or more imminent the danger, the greater the stress reaction.

[b] evaluations of danger or dangers often were not made until the evaluer had experience of particular situations of danger.

[c] those with prior experience of danger of frightening situations were amongst the first to want to take avoidance actions or who were subject to stress reactions.

[d] stress reactions were heightened where there were no effective measures to deal with potential danger. Physiological reaction was far less with experienced than with inexperienced performers.

[e] some situations without danger or potential danger can still cause stress reactions and effects. Personal insult, questioning of intelligence, courage or

integrity, rejection and other social attempts to manipulate people through words come into this category.

The individuals most affected are those who are anxiety prone, test anxious, aggressive or needing social approval. Other types of personality may be affected in addition to the above.

Factors Producing Stress in Trampolining

The factors which produce stress in trampolining for the pupil are:

[a] the unusual body positions and rotational and twisting movements to be learned;

[b] the physical dangers of failure;

[c] competition and training;

[d] fatigue.

1 *Unusual Body Positions*

In everyday life most people experience two body positions, vertical and horizontal. Any loss of these positions is resisted. The whole essence of trampolining is to pass through a whole variety of different positions, at varying speeds of rotation and height, in more than one plane. Our past informs us that vertical and horizontal are the only safe positions. Thus the pupil is not only involved in learning physical skills, which is enough of a problem, but in learning them in a variety of body positions with all the attendant visual and equilibrium problems. There is a strong tendency to try to achieve the skills without too much deviation from what is known. This may lead to anticipation faults and consequent loss of performance and thus danger. At low levels of height and skill this

may be sufficient but it will build problems later.

2 *Physical Dangers of Failure*

These are very real, and include landing on the frame with danger of bruising, falling off with danger of further injuries, and falling on the bed with danger of damage to the body joints, including the very real danger of damage to the neck or spine from inverted landings. Fear of these dangers can cause the pupil to be tense physically and mentally with consequent loss of performance.

3 *Competition and Training*

When the competition is for a World Championship, National Championship or other important event, or the performer has to allay the wrath or disappointment of a parent or coach, the stress reaction can be quite high. There is often outward display of nervousness and skill can be to a certain extent replaced by determination, the performer concentrating on power rather than skill. Other manifestations of stress are anger with oneself, the coach or parents due to lack of success. This lack of success can be due to the demands of the parent or coach or the fault of the performer. It can lead to a fierce striving to prove the stressor wrong. The hormone influence due to anger may give greater physical strength and possibly enhanced motor activity but not necessarily greater discriminatory powers. The performer may not realise that performance has diminished and refuses to stop activity even when failing. Overt pressures for success from a parent or coach, constant demands for more work, higher difficulty or the need to beat the nearest rival, may lead to under achieving feelings or guilt in the pupil. In consequence a higher work rate is entered into, more work-outs are arranged and fatigue and diminished concentration become additional stressors.

4 *Fatigue*

Fatigue leads to a lessening of performance through diminished motor response and loss of power, endurance and the ability to concentrate. During highly skilled performance or the learning of a complex skill, the sustained attention on the task and the relevant sensory stimuli will be further diminished. More attention will be paid to irrelevant stimuli as concentration lessens. These stimuli may be in the form of people talking, or moving, spotters not paying attention or noises which are not normally heard by the performer when a high alertness or concentration level is being maintained.

Fatigue on the trampoline leads to decreasing efficiency the longer a skill is performed. Fatigue may not be apparent, because of the responsive rebound of the equipment. The performer may however be having to work harder to maintain height. The total amount of power available for height is also used for rotation, so any falling off in power will lessen the chances of success. The highly skilled trampolinist has an optimum working height and power output. Any lessening of either or both of these will diminish efficiency. Loss of efficiency plus determination or anger is potentially dangerous.

There may be less obvious signs that a pupil is not in the best condition to perform skillfully. The pupil may be under medication or have emotional problems. Calling out in sleep or a noticeable nervous tic may be signs of stress and should be taken into account by all concerned with the performer's well-being.

Stress Factors Affecting the Coach

The performer is not the only one who is affected by stress. The coach is affected for a number of reasons; some of them are:

[a] responsibility for pupils;

[b] fear of accidents and loss of reputation and job;

[c] problems of introducing new moves and removing support safely;

[d] conflict with pupils, parents or employers during training periods leading up to competitions.

Some of the above stresses on the coach may not be removed easily. However, coaches can take action to try to ensure that they are better prepared in their roles to avoid unnecessary stress, as follows.

[a] Make sure that all techniques used are sound in principle and practice.

[b] Do not become angry with pupils and belittle them publicly.

[c] Do not blame pupils for failure.

[d] Make use of low but stimulating stress.

[e] Do not work pupils when both coach and pupil are tired.

[f] Recognise that each pupil is unique and work to the strengths of each pupil.

[g] Do not become too emotionally involved.

[h] Do not over-react to specific personality traits of which you do not approve in a pupil.

[i] Understand and use a basic knowledge of psychology.

[j] Try to get a true picture of each pupil and use it as a basis for intelligent teaching.

All coaches should remember that courage or 'guts' are expendable items, reasonable demands are more likely to be realised. Enthusiastic ignorance is a quality to be avoided.

Signs of Stress in the Athlete or Competitor

As stated previously, stress can have good or bad effects. It is important therefore that the coach can recognise the signs of stress, especially those signs which will indicate that the stress factor is too high and must be alleviated to avoid both short- and long-term deleterious effects. Many coaches, in ignorance, persist in attempts to improve the performance of pupils when poor performance is caused by a factor which cannot be alleviated by persistent application by both coach and performer.

Whilst recognising that each pupil is an individual and will behave in ways that are consistent with personality types, some behaviour patterns might result from stress rather than personality.

The following characteristic indications of stress will possibly help coaches, both in training and competition, to recognise when there is too high a level of stress. Many competitors in trampolining lose moves which they have been successfully performing, often for a long time. It seems to be a mystery why this happens, but it does, and mostly to competitors. It can lead to accidents, and often leads to the abandoning of competitive trampolining. This loss of moves may be a warning of something basically wrong with the training programme, the amount of competition, the level of pressure from the coach, the expectations of the pupil or some other factor which could and should be recognised.

There are several well-known signs of stress, the most commonly experienced one being 'butterflies' in the stomach. A number of other signs may be recognised, and the following may help the coach and performer to overcome them or at least not to worry too much about them.

Mild Stress, Physical Signs

Dry mouth, butterflies, frequent visits to the toilet, heartbeat obvious, jumpiness, tingling of scalp, loss of appetite, slight shaking of the hands.

Severe Stress, Physical Signs

Dry mouth, pallor, palpitations of the heart, deep breathing, tenseness, increased muscle tone, frequent visits to the toilet, noticeable shaking of the hands, vomiting, sweating on the brow and hands, jumpiness on hearing noises.

Physiological Signs

Talkativeness, feeling of tension, change of mood, easily upset by change of routine or programme, last minute need to practise, repetitive questioning about time, order of performance, desire to change competitive routine even at the last stage before competition.

If the coach sees any of the above it is wise to try to keep the pupil calm, mainly by showing calmness oneself and acting in a matter of fact way. Any signs of stress or anxiety in the coach are easily picked up by the competitor and often cause more agitation.

15

The Tariff System

In trampolining the score for competition routines is compiled by adding together the score for form (style) and difficulty. The difficulty of a skill is measured by a numerical system related to the number of somersaults and twists in each skill. This system was originated by an American named Bob Bollinger and was named the 'axial rotation system'. It has been universally adopted to denote the difficulty (tariff) rating of each skill.

Below are the simple principles under which the system operates. It will operate whether the performer is taking off from the feet, stomach, seat or back. In each instance the number of degrees is totalled up for both somersault and twist (if any) for each of the ten skills of a competitive routine. This total is then added to the total for form. The form score is the sum of the middle three scores out of those awarded by the five form judges. Each judge can deduct up to 0.5 out of a possible 1.0 for each of the ten skills in a competitive routine.

Tariffing Principles

1	Skills with no rotation or less than 90 degrees of somersault rotation (lateral axis).	0.1
2	For each 90 degrees ($\frac{1}{4}$ somersault) of rotation.	0.1
3	For each 180 degrees of rotation about the longitudinal axis (half twist).	0.1
4	For 360 or more degrees of somersault *without* twist	
5	For 720 degrees or more somersault *with twist*, when performed in the *piked or straight position an extra mark is added on*	0.1

Examples

[a]	Straight jump/tucked jump/piked jump/piked straddle jump	0.0
[b]	Feet to seat drop	0.0
[c]	Seat to feet	0.0
[d]	Feet to front drop	0.1
[e]	Front to feet	0.1
[f]	Jump with $\frac{1}{2}$ twist	0.1
[g]	Jump with full twist	0.2
[h]	$\frac{1}{2}$ Twist to front drop	0.2
[i]	Back drop, $\frac{1}{2}$ twist to feet	0.2
[j]	$\frac{3}{4}$ Back somersault (t,p,s)	0.3
[k]	Back drop to front drop	0.2

[l] Back drop, full twist to back (Cat twist)	0.2

[m] Back drop, forward rotation with $\frac{1}{2}$ twist to back drop	0.3

[n] Back somersault (tucked)	0.4
Back somersault (piked)	0.5
Back somersault (straight)	0.5

[o] Double back somersault (tucked)	0.8
Double back somersault (piked)	0.9
Double back somersault (straight)	0.9

[p] Back somersault (tucked) to seat	0.4
Back pullover (t,p,s)	0.3
Back somersault (piked) to seat	0.5
Back somersault (straight) to seat	0.5

[q] $1\frac{1}{4}$ Front somersaults (tucked)	0.4
$1\frac{1}{4}$ Front somersaults (piked)	0.5
$1\frac{1}{4}$ Front somersaults (straight)	0.5

[r] Front somersault with $\frac{1}{2}$ twist (barani) (tucked, piked, or straight)	0.5

[s] Front somersault with $1\frac{1}{2}$ twists (rudolph) (tucked, piked, or straight)	0.7

[t] Back somersault with 1 twist	0.6

[u] Back somersault with 2 twists	0.8

[v] $1\frac{1}{4}$ Front somersaults with $\frac{1}{2}$ twist (e.g. ball out barani (t,p,s)	0.6

[w] Double front somersault with $\frac{1}{2}$ twist (fliffus) (tucked)	0.9
Double front somersault with $\frac{1}{2}$ twist (fliffus) (piked)	1.0
Double front somersault with $\frac{1}{2}$ twist (fliffus) (straight)	1.0

[x] Triple front somersault, with $\frac{1}{2}$ twist (fliffus) (tucked)	1.3
Triple front somersault, with $\frac{1}{2}$ twist (fliffus) (piked)	1.4

For competition the coach needs to know all the difficulty values or how to work them out. He needs to realise that there is a tariff for the descent to a back drop (this is a skill in itself) and another value for the 90° rotation to feet (a separate skill). All routines must end on the feet. Repeating the same skill results in loss of tariff for the repeated move. A piked front somersault and a tucked front somersault are considered as different skills. The difficulty rating is checked before and during the routine by the difficulty judges. Many routines are given incorrect difficulty ratings by the coach through lack of necessary knowledge and possibly poorly designed routines for his competitors.

Note on routines (see opposite page)

A competition consists of a compulsory, a voluntary and a second voluntary routine for the ten finalists. All routines are composed of ten skills. Until recently all compulsories consisted of ten prescribed skills. Recently, the International Trampoline Federation, in an attempt to make competitions more attractive to the public, has changed the format of compulsory routines for International Championships. The routine will now consist of five compulsory and five optional skills.

16

The Development of Routines

For the serious or competitive trampolinist it is necessary to learn routines consisting of a number of skills performed in sequence. Without this ability no trampolinist will be able to take part in competitions. For success in the proficiency scheme it is also necessary to learn routines in order to get ahead and earn the badges. This book has so far set out the methods for learning many moves on the trampoline as individual moves. This next short section will give an outline of the methods which can be used to build routines for competition.

A series of routines is included which are progressively more difficult and graded in such a way that with a little time and effort spent on practice it should be possible to keep progressing from routine to routine. At times this may be slow or it may be necessary to try a different order of skills to overcome a sticking point. Let us look at the routines and see how one can progress.

Graded Routines

These routines are suitable for a learner making a first attempt at routines and then progressing forwards from an eight contact routine to ten contact routines and then increasing the difficulty from 0.3 through to 7.0. This will provide graded progress with plenty of challenge for about three to four years or even more with constant work at the sport. The normal pupil will never reach even the 7.0 level unless he is very interested in competition and becomes a performer of a

level of junior international or open Divisional champion. However, it is good to have examples of routines which can aid progress to this level. At the end are examples of high tariff voluntary routines currently used by the top British competitors. Notice that the Ladies' routine has at present no triple somersaults, possibly since there is no need to get into even higher tariffs. The Men's routine has one triple somersault and the rest are double somersaults with twists. In the Ladies' routine there are all double somersaults, two of which do not have twists.

With regard to International level competition, with a chance of winning, it can be seen from the routines presented that the difficulty level must be very high and of good form. Some competitors can manage high difficult manoeuvres but not very good form and some can produce very good form but never reach superior difficulty. At every European and World Championship there is a male performer who has a very high level of difficulty but cannot make the whole routine. The level of difficulty always creates interest, which disappears as soon as the inability to complete the routine is obvious. The final routine in the series gives a real comparison between the level of those just entering serious competition and those at the very top level.

Pupils can start on routines as soon as they have learned one skill. That is they can repeat the move in what is called 'swingtime'. This helps to sharpen the mind and gives practice in the slightly different timing of two landings for repetition of skills. At low level it gives increased interest and a greater training effect than performing a move just once, and thus increases the return to the pupil of the work on the trampoline. As more and more moves are learned, simple routines can be built up using the moves in different orders as the pupil progresses, thus giving versatility of performance, most important for the serious or competitive performer.

The British Trampoline Federation has published a Proficiency Scheme which provides a ready-made graded scheme of work for those interested in working through the sport from basic levels to very high levels over a number of years. There are badges of attainment for all levels, which enable the pupil to show to all the level of skill attained, by a regular examination by a qualified examiner.

Let us look at the first three routines shown on the series. This will take the pupil from a routine using only the basic skills and having a tariff of 0.3 to a tariff using the basic skills and two tucked somersaults reaching a tariff of 1.5.

The Learning of Routines

The learning of routines will be easier if some systematic approach is made to avoid wasting time and effort and the disappointment of failure. In most instances an advanced competitor will have a number of routines in practice and it is fairly simple to add different moves at stages of progress. This may mean a re-arrangement of some of the moves or simply changing the first and last moves.

For the beginner at learning routines it is usually easier to start with one or two moves and then add extra moves at the start of the routine. One new move at the beginning is easier to remember than having to think about four or five moves and then having to add one more. It may also prove wise to

practise the new move to be added with only the one that follows it so that even before putting the whole group together the new move has been practised with the following move. The subsequent ones have already been practised together.

During training it may be necessary to separate out moves from the routine for more attention to performance. This is better done in small blocks of two or three so that a move is not practised too much in isolation without attention to the slightly different techniques needed for success in swingtime performance. Much attention will be needed on landing and take-off positions and techniques for using the arms, due to the great effect they will have on the performance of the skills following.

Basic Principles

1 Build progressively.

2 Put in only what you have mastered.

3 Increase difficulty by adding skills at the start or end of the routine after practice in those positions.

4 Have a new routine ready for competition use well before you need it.

5 Build on consistent performance rather than hope.

6 Remember that an extra .1 from each form judge for each move means 3.0 on the total: an extra 3.0 on tariff is possibly 2 years work.

The requirements of a competitive routine are to display the performer's best form and control of individual movement at a consistent height. The coach must guide the performer in using increasing difficulty without detracting from the overall quality of the routine. Individuals vary in their ability to handle increasing difficulty; there is no way to develop. Here are some examples of possible developments. The BTF Proficiency Scheme offers good examples of progressive demands on skill development.

The first routine has only three moves with a tariff value. There is very little rotation in the routine, mainly shaped jumps, a twisting move and then a seat drop giving a different landing position, although a very easy one. The final move is a front drop followed by a rotation to feet, which both have a tariff of one. The other tariffed move is the half twist jump which also has a tariff value of one.

1	Piked straddle jump	0.0
2	Seat drop	0.0
3	To feet	0.0
4	Tucked jump	0.0
5	$\frac{1}{2}$ Twist jump	0.1
6	Piked jump	0.0
7	Front drop	0.1
8	To feet	0.1
Routine 1		**0.3**

The second routine has a far greater tariff value and includes a somersault. This means that the pupil must be at the stage of performing a somersault. The first somersault usually learned is the front somersault. It is put at the end of the routine so that, if not successfully performed, it does not spoil the rest of the routine. The routine also includes variations on the basic jumps and landing positions by adding twists to a number of moves including twists to and from landing positions other than the feet. Notice that the somersault is in the tucked position, normally the easiest position in which to learn a somersault. It is also placed at the end of the routine so that failure in this, the most difficult of the moves in the routine, does not mean disaster for the competitor.

1	Full twist jump	0.2
2	Piked straddle jump	0.0
3	$\frac{1}{2}$ Twist to seat	0.1
4	$\frac{1}{2}$ Twist to feet	0.1
5	$\frac{1}{2}$ Twist jump	0.1
6	Piked jump	0.0
7	Back drop	0.1
8	$\frac{1}{2}$ Twist to feet	0.2
9	Tucked jump	0.0
10	Front somersault (tucked)	0.4
Routine 2		**1.2**

The third routine has two somersaults, one at the start and one at the end. Notice that the front somersault is the last move and the new somersault is at the front. Although there could be a problem of the back somersault not being performed well and the routine being spoiled, it is still safer to put the move where there is no problem from the performance of another move. The front somersault is at the end of the routine because it is also more difficult to put a blind move like this at the beginning of a routine.

1	Back somersault (Tucked)	0.4
2	Seat drop	0.0
3	½ Twist to feet	0.1
4	Full twist jump	0.2
5	Piked straddle jump	0.0
6	Back drop	0.1
7	½ Twist to feet	0.2
8	½ Twist jump	0.1
9	Tucked jump	0.0
10	Front somersault (Tucked)	0.4

| **Routine 3** | | 1.5 |

The second and third routines have been used as compulsory routines for the British Schools and the British Under 11 competitions respectively. They are low tariff to try to encourage the performers to show better form and to enable more competitors to enter. If the compulsory routine is too difficult it does tend to keep competitors away, which does not help the development of competitive trampolining. At schools competition and under thirteen levels it is necessary to try to get as many involved as possible so that they get early experience at competitive work without finding the levels too high. Later on, a moderate increase in difficulty is used to try to keep the emphasis on good form.

Routines 4 and 5 show the use of shaped somersaults, piked and tucked, in order to increase tariff but not to change the routine too much. Routine 4 still has simple jumps in it and the tariff is 3.0. It is comparatively simple, has no body landings to make the regaining of height a problem and is within the compass of a relatively inexperienced but accomplished performer (i.e. a pupil who shows an obvious aptitude for the sport). For the first time a twisting somersault is used, the barani. It can be seen that gradually the complexity of skill is increasing as the routines are changed.

Routine 5, although of only 0.2 difficulty more than Routine 4, is much more difficult to perform. There are six somersaults, two of which have landings other than on the feet, involving the regaining of height from these landings. This routine will only be performed well after a lot of practice, and, what is more, the increase in tariff is very little for the extra work. Although it is necessary to move ahead it may be found that the loss of form mark is greater than the gain in tariff mark. This will always be a problem as the difficulty of a routine is increased, and it means that to keep competition success going, large increases in tariff should be avoided if they mean a subsequent loss in form mark. It is better to have more practice with the extra difficulty than to put it into the competition too soon.

1	Back somersault (Straight)	0.5
2	Barani (Straight)	0.5
3	Piked straddle jump	0.0

4 Back somersault (Piked)		0.5
5 Barani (Tucked)		0.5
6 Piked jump		0.0
7 Back somersault (Tucked)		0.4
8 $2\frac{1}{2}$ Twist jump		0.1
9 Tucked jump		0.0
10 Front somersault (Piked)		0.5
Routine 4		**3.0**

1 Back somersault (Straight)		0.5
2 Back somersault (Tucked)		0.4
3 Barani (Straight)		0.5
4 Back somersault (Tucked) to seat		0.4
5 $\frac{1}{2}$ Twist to feet		0.1
6 Piked jump		0.0
7 Back somersault (Piked)		0.5
8 Tucked jump		0.0
9 $1\frac{1}{4}$ Back somersault (Tucked)		0.5
10 Back pullover (Piked)		0.3
Routine 5		**3.2**

Routine 6 shows a large increase in tariff over the last one. Again it uses back and front take-offs but the skills from these landing positions are more difficult. The cody is introduced from the stomach landing and the ball out barani from the back. The landings for these moves are critical and much practice will be needed to ensure that the use of these skills does not detract too much from the gaining of marks. Cody somersaults have tended to disappear from routines in the past few years but the move is often used in compulsory routines and is a valid skill from the point of view of the skills capable of performance on the trampoline. It will be noticed in the routines shown that there are not many front and back landing skills after the lower level work. They do come into use to increase easily the difficulty at one stage. They disappear again as the demands of competition make it obvious that a series of feet-to-feet skills give better sighting of the bed and thus better security. Looking at the routine, it can be seen that changing the three-quarter front somersault to a one and three-quarter front somersault would increase the tariff to 4.6. It is, however, a new phase in development, the introduction of multiple somersaults. Difficulty can still be increased but the routine will need to be all somersaults of different shapes and will usually need the introduction of multiple twists.

Routine 7 has a large increase in tariff over Routine 6, almost a whole mark. A multiple twisting somersault is brought in, the one and a half twisting front somersault which is the same tariff as the one and three-quarter front somersault mentioned in the previous routine. In fact the previous routine could be increased from 4.2, by the introduction of a one and three-quarter front somersault, to 4.6, and then by the introduction of the rudolf (one and a half twisting front) instead of the piked straddle jump, to 5.3. This would necessitate a rearranging of the order of skills for the easier performance of the routine. It could be done by putting a back somersault after the cody to gain some possible lost height followed by the rudolf. A second back somersault could be used, followed by the barani. The last part of the routine would still be the same.

Routine 7 shows a different method of increasing tariff by introducing a multiple twisting front somersault, the rudolf, and by alternating a front and a back somersault take-off to try to get around the problem of loss of height through similar take-off directions. The use of a simple front somersault at the end of the routine is a method of easily having a 0.5 tariff move to increase tariff. Since there is no move following the front there is no possibility of further loss of height. The routine now includes four twisting somersaults.

1 $\frac{3}{4}$ Back somersault (Straight)		0.3
2 Cody (Tucked)		0.5
3 Piked straddle jump		0.0
4 Back somersault (Straight)		0.5
5 Barani (Piked)		0.5
6 Back somersault (Piked)		0.5
7 Back somersault with full twist		0.6
8 Back somersault (Tucked)		0.4
9 $\frac{3}{4}$ Front somersault (Straight)		0.3
10 Ball-out barani (Tucked)		0.6
Routine 6		4.2

1 Back somersault (Straight)		0.5
2 Back somersault with full twist		0.6
3 $1\frac{1}{4}$ Back somersault (Piked)		0.6
4 Back pullover (Piked)		0.3
5 Barani (Piked)		0.5
6 Back somersault (Piked)		0.5
7 Rudolf		0.7
8 Back somersault (Tucked)		0.4
9 Barani (Tucked)		0.5
10 Front somersault (Piked)		0.5
Routine 7		5.1

Routine 8 has still four twisting somersaults but has brought in a multiple somersault, the one and three-quarter front somersault. The front somersault piked is still at the end of the routine for extra easy tariff, but the routine is quite difficult and no-one without considerable jumping experience over two to three years will be able to handle it unless very talented. The ordinary performer without regular frequent training will not be at this level, if ever.

Routine 9 with a tariff of 6.2 has moved a stage further in complexity of movement. It has the first fliffus (a twisting double somersault) at the beginning and a one and three-quarter front with a fairly difficult ending move, the rudolf ball out (one and one quarter front somersault from back landing with one and one half twists). One can now understand the need for shortened special names.

Further development in linking twisting somersaults, the introduction of one or two one and three-quarter front somersaults should steadily lead to the use of a fliffus, initially, at the beginning of a routine, where it should be possible to obtain the best take-off, consistently, to control the first double somersault with twist (usually the half out).

1	Back somersault (Straight)	0.5
2	Barani (Piked)	0.5
3	Back somersault with full twist	0.6
4	Rudolf	0.7
5	Back somersault (Piked)	0.5
6	Barani (Tucked)	0.5
7	Back somersault (Tucked)	0.4
8	$1\frac{3}{4}$ Front somersault (Tucked)	0.7
9	Ball-out barani (Tucked)	0.6
10	Front somersault (Piked)	0.5
Routine 8		**5.5**

1	$\frac{1}{2}$ Out fliffus (Tucked)	0.9
2	Barani (Piked)	0.5
3	Back somersault (Piked)	0.5

4	Back somersault with full twist	0.6
5	Rudolf	0.7
6	Back somersault (Straight)	0.5
7	Barani (Tucked)	0.5
8	Back somersault (Tucked)	0.4
9	$1\frac{3}{4}$ Front somersault (Piked)	0.8
10	Rudolf ball-out	0.8
Routine 9		**6.2**

Routines 10 and 11 are even more complex without very large increases in tariff. Routine 10 has three multiple somersaults and Routine 11 has four, three of them in sequence. Notice that the double back has gone from the last move, where it is in a safe place, to third move after two other double somersaults. This represents an increase in difficulty of performance without an increase in tariff, but is necessary for progress to routines of even greater tariff.

At this point individuals will vary greatly in their approach to increases in difficulty. A balance of backward and forward movements, tucked and piked, with early and late twists should be developed. Alternate forwards and backwards movements often help the ready flow and rhythm of a routine—provided that the control of direction of take-off is accurate. At this stage tariff increases are very small and the main attention is given towards consolidation of skills, both individual and combination, to help better and safer development of a pupil's potential. The coach must be aware, at this level of difficulty, what combinations are possible, what the pupil can handle best and in what order. Individual attention to each pupil is very necessary with discussion between pupil and coach playing a large part in accurate assessment of when and how to progress. Some very young pupils will be getting up to this level of difficulty and may have problems in giving accurate verbal responses, which are useful to both coach and pupil.

1	$\frac{1}{2}$ Out fliffus (Piked)	1.0
2	$\frac{1}{2}$ Out fliffus (Tucked)	0.9
3	Back somersault (Straight)	0.5
4	Barani (Piked)	0.5
5	Back somersault with full twist	0.6
6	Rudolf	0.7
7	Back somersault (Piked)	0.5
8	Barani (Tucked)	0.5
9	Back somersault (Tucked)	0.4
10	Double back somersault (Tucked)	0.3
Routine 10		**6.4**

1	$\frac{1}{2}$ Out fliffus (Piked)	1.0
2	$\frac{1}{2}$ Out fliffus (Tucked)	0.9
3	Double back somersault (Tucked)	0.8
4	Barani (Piked)	0.5
5	Back somersault with full twist	0.6
6	Rudolf	0.7
7	Back somersault (Piked)	0.5
8	Back somersault (Tucked)	0.4
9	$1\frac{3}{4}$ Front somersault (Piked)	0.8
10	Rudolf ball-out	0.8
Routine 11		**7.0**

Increases above this level are hard earned as it requires multi-twisting skills and/or multi-somersault skills to be brought into the routine for only small increases in tariff value. New skills, normally brought in at the beginning of a routine, may require reorganisation of existing skills. A small change may have little benefit to the difficulty immediately but may provide a better basis for future routines.

Trampoline Terminology

Terms used in the sport, which may be used freely amongst those 'in the know' and are very puzzling to those just overhearing them, are given. All trampoline 'experts' should have these at their fingertips.

Adolf Three and one half twisting front somersault.

Anchor bars The metal or plastic parts to which each end of the cable or spring is fixed from the bed to the frame.

Baby fliffus Forwards half twist into a back somersault from the back landing position.

Back Abbreviation for back somersault.

Back pullover Back drop backward rotation to stomach or feet.

Ball out One and a quarter front somersault from the back landing position to land on the feet. Also used to describe all forward somersaults originating from the back landing position.

Ball out half out (Ball out fliffus) Two and a quarter front somersault off the back with half twist in the final somersault.

Ball out rudi out As above but with one and a half twists in the final somersault.

Barani A trampoline movement in which the body completes a front somersault with a half twist in such a way that the performer can see the bed throughout the entire movement.

Barani in Double front somersault with a half twist in the first somersault.

Barani out Double front somersault with a half twist in the second somersault.

Barrel roll A side somersault from feet to feet.

Bed The jumping area of the trampoline. Can be solid nylon, webbed nylon in 24 mm, 12 mm, 6 mm mesh. There are also beds in woven string.

Blind Where the performer does not see the bed until the point of contact or later.

Bluch Front drop backward rotation about the lateral axis with half twist to front drop.

Break Arresting the recoil of the bed.

Cast Aerial sideways movement across the bed.

Cat twist Back drop full twist without somersault rotation to back drop. Also double/triple/quadruple cat twist.

Check Arresting the recoil of the bed.

Check list Series of skills providing a work sheet or measure of progress.

Cody A term describing back or front somersault movements from a front drop position take-off (named after Dale Cote, Alhambra California, who was the first to use them).

Corkscrew As above but with one and a half twists.

Comp A trampoline competition or a compulsory routine.

Barrel

Corpse Flat back landing in a back drop.

Cradle Back drop forward rotation half twist early or late to back drop.

Crash dive Three-quarter front somersault straight from feet to back landing position.

Crash mat Mattress used for landings whilst the pupil is learning skills. About 6 ft. × 4 ft. × 8 ins (1.8 × 1.2 × 0.2m). Made from plastic foam with a cover.

De-Sync Judge Judge in a competition recording the lack of synchronisation in a routine.

Devil Back drop forward rotation with three and a half twists to back drop (named after John Devlin Belfast).

Dismount A means of getting off the trampoline.

Double Usually any double somersault.

Double back Back somersault performed twice in the air with no landing in between.

Double bouncing Two persons jumping on the trampoline at the same time.

Double full A double twisting back somersault.

Doubles As above.

Double twister A double twisting back somersault.

Fliffus A twisting double somersault. Derived from flip and twist, sometimes fliffis, plural fliffes (pronounced fliffees). Often shortened to fliffs.

Flip American term for somersault.

Form The grace and precision with which the performer executes skills.

Foot thrust The action of the feet against the bed. The direction of the foot thrust is directly related to the amount and direction of rotation. Newton's Third Law (equal and opposite).

Frame pads Covering for the frame of the trampoline to soften the effect of any impact upon the frame.

Free Denoting no set body position in a skill.

Free bounce A straight jump with no other shape or movement included.

Front A forward somersault.

Full Refers to a 360° twist in any somersault.

Full in Denotes a full twist in the first somersault of a twisting double somersault.

Full out Denotes a full twist in the second somersault of a twisting double somersault.

Gain Movement along the trampoline bed in the opposite direction to that of the somersault.

Half in half out A double somersault with one half twist in the first somersault and one half twist in the second.

Harness The belt used for learning somersaults.

Hip thrust Action of displacement of the hips to initiate somersaults, can be forward or backward. Hip displacement would be a better term. Thrust denotes too much power in the action.

Jona back Early half twist from feet into a back somersault.

Kaboom An onomatopaeic term describing a front or back landing in which two contacts are made. The second part to land is then accelerated past the first part to land to give rotation in the original direction of the front or back landing.

Kill Flexing the knees and hips on contact to absorb the recoil of the springs, thereby keeping the body in contact with the bed.

Kip Action of a second person on the bed controlling the rebound of the bed to increase, stabilise or decrease it.

Knee drop A simple basic landing position on the knees with the body in the upright position. Although simple can cause problems with the back if it is not held straight.

Knock-out system Man-to-man competition where one competitor must defeat an opponent before moving on to the next round.

Landing platform Extension added to each end of the trampoline supporting a mattress secured over a resilient frame. Standard competition requirement.

Layout An extended body position during a somersault.

Lean Moving the body in the direction of rotation. Results in travel.

Lift Going for height.

Log roll A front drop full twist to front drop.

Lost When the performer is disorientated in relation to the surroundings.

Miller A triple twisting double back done with a two and one half twist in the first somersault and a half in the second. Named after Wayne Miller (World Champion) who first performed it.

Mount Two meanings for this: either the first move in a routine or the means of getting on the trampoline (opposite of dismount).

Open To come out of a tuck or pike into a straighter position ready for landing: non-tucked or piked but not straight body position.

Out bounce The final jump before coming to rest after a routine. One out bounce is allowed at the end of a routine to gain stability.

Overthrow Putting too much rotation into a somersault. Usually when adding more twist.

Pick-up A gatherer of information.

Pike A position where the legs are at a right-angle, or less, in relation to the trunk.

Pit tramp A trampoline set into the ground so that the frame edges are at ground level. Used mainly in public 'pay as you go' trampoline parks. The disadvantage is that the air displaced has to be forced out round the side of the trampoline and slows the rebound.

Plenty of top A lot of lift with all the somersault rotation at the top.

Porpoise Forward somersault from back drop to back drop.

Psyche up To prepare psychologically for a competition or routine.

Puck A body shape mid-way between tucked and piked. It is used for fliffes and enables a performer to somersault relatively quickly whilst twisting relatively slowly.

Pull over A three-quarter somersault from back drop rotating backwards to the feet.

Randolph Forward single somersault with two and a half twists. Also **Randy**.

Randolph (Randy) Ball out Forward two and a quarter somersault from the back landing position.

Rig The safety harness.

Rob Roy Cradle with two and a half twists.

Roller Seat drop horizontal full twist to seat drop.

Roller stands Inverted tee-shaped stands with roller castors upon which the trampoline can be moved around, both folded and open.

Routine The series of skills performed for competitive trampolining. Normally ten skills.

Rudi out A double somersault with one and a half twists in the second somersault.

Rudi in A double somersault with one and a half twists in the first somersault.

Rudolf A single front somersault with one and a half twists.

Safety sides Extra bars at the side of the trampoline for the coach to stand on whilst ready to step in and support.

Scoop Bending the knees at the take-off for a back somersault so that the hips move forwards too low, height is then lost.

Set A compulsory routine.

Side A side somersault.

Slide out The action of opening from a tucked or piked position whilst keeping the arms in contact with the legs, giving the appearance that the legs are slid through the hands.

Sommy A somersault.

Spotter One who stands by ready to catch or support. A skill performed on the spot.

Stand in Also one who stands by ready to catch or support.

Swingtime Skills performed consecutively without any free bounce in between.

Swivel hips Seat drop half twist to seat drop.

Synchro Synchronised trampolining by two performers on two different trampolines.

Tariff The mathematically assessed difficulty rating of a skill. 0.1 for each 90° of somersault, 0.1 for each 180° of twist, extra 0.1 for layout and piked body shapes in single somersaults or double somersaults.

Throw in mat A small mattress used if a pupil is seen to be making an unsure landing.

Tramp Trampoline.

Travel Movement along the bed in the same direction in which the movement is being performed.

Triffus Triple somersault with twist.

Triple Triple somersault.

Triple full Triple twisting somersault.

Tuck Body position with the knees drawn up to the chest and the hands grasping the shins.

Turnover Forward rotation not necessarily a somersault.

Turntable Front drop sideways rotation to land in another front drop.

Twister A twisting somersault.

Twisting belt Harness with concentric rings to enable the performer to twist and somersault at the same time whilst being supported.

Vol A voluntary routine.

Wrap To pull in the arms to the chest to accelerate speed of twist.

Index

absorption of force 142
acceleration 143
    angular 144
    law of 141
    potential 18
accident 15
accidents, causes of 150
action-making process 151
adolf 185
age of participants 156, 160
analysis of skill 168–9
angular, acceleration 143
    momentum 144
    momentum, transfer of 149
    velocity 143
ankle injuries 158
arching 21
arm, action 17
    swing 16
axes of rotation 147
axis 144

baby fliffus, cradle back 90
back drop, from one leg 33
    full twist to feet 37, 66
    half twist to feet 35, 66
    piked 32
    straight 31
    support 64
    to front drop 36
    tucked 32
back in full out fliffus 130
back kaboom 95
    support 77
back pullover, bomb type 49
    support 66
    to stomach 50
    to feet with leg kick 50
    tucked (first stages) 48
back somersault, piked 52
    straight 53
    straight with half twist 97
    support 69–71
    tucked 51
    tucked to seat drop 54

with double twist 103
with full twist 99
with full twist in safety harness 76
with full twist support (hand) 75
ball out, barani 89
    barani straight 91
    support 78
    tucked from forward turnover or crash dive 88
barani 96
    in piked 122
    in tucked 121
    out fliffus piked 119
    out fliffus straight 120
    out fliffus tucked 118
    support 119, 122
basic first aid 157
basic jumping skills 16
basic principles (the learning of routines) 178
bed, checking 14
    types 13
body positions, unusual 172
bouncing 30
broken limbs 159
bruises 157

cast 185
castors 13
cat twist 185
centre of mass 143
centrifugal force 142
check 185
check list 185
coach, qualities of 170
coaching course 15
cody 83, 185
    kick 83
    preparation for with hand support 79, 80
comp 185
competition 15
competitiveness 152
contributory causes of accidents 152
conservation of momentum 148
corkscrew 40, 185
corpse 186
counterforce 141

cradle 186
  early twist 39
  late twist 40
crash dive 85
  half twist into 86, 87
  support 71
crash mat 186
  use of 57
cuts 157

damage of equipment 14
dangers of failure 172
decision making 150–1
de-sync judge 186
development of routines 177
devil 186
dismount 186
displacement, rotation by 146
distribution, of practice 166
double 186
  back 186
  back somersault 109; piked 111; straight 112
  ball out with half twist out 137
  bouncing 186
  front piked with one and a half twists out 128
  front tucked with one and a half twists 127
  full 186
  twister 186
doubles 186

eccentric force, lateral axis 147
  longitudinal axis 146
energy, stored 142
environmental factors 162
equipment 13
  checking 13
ergonomic cycle 162, 163

fatigue 173
flat back drop from feet 31
fliffus 186
flip 186
foot thrust 186
force 183
  absorption of 142
  eccentric 146
forearm injury 158
form 186
forward rotation from the back landing position
  (ball out kick) 87
forward turnover from back to back (porpoise) 88
frame 13
  pads 186
free bounce 186
front 186

front drop, half twist to feet 34
  full twist to feet 37
  piked 30
  straight 27
  support 63
  to back drop 38
  tucked 29
front kaboom 94
front one and a quarter somersault from back
  with one and a half twists (rudi ball out) 92
front somersault, hand support 68
  one and a half twists (rudi) 101
  piked 46
  straight 47
  to seat drop (tucked) 44
  tucked 45
  with full twist 100
  with full twist support (hand) 74
  with two and a half twists (randolf) 103
full in 186
  back out fliffus 128
  full out fliffus 132
  half out 133
  one and a half fliffus (full in rudi out) 135
full out 186
full twist, to back drop 36
  to back drop with support 65
  to front drop 36

gain 186
graded routines 177
graphics 164
gyration, radius of 144

habit 152
half in half out 186
  fliffus 124
  piked 126
half in one and a half twisting front out fliffus 136
half in one and three quarter front somersault
  tucked 123
half twist, into three quarter (crash dive) front
  somersault 86
  to back drop 35
  to back drop with support 65
  to front drop 55
  to seat drop 25
half turn into three quarter front somersault
  support 72
hall 13
hands and knees drop forward turnover, to back
  drop 43
  tucked to seat drop 43
  with support 67
hand holds for supporting 63

hand support behind back 69
harness 186
head injury 158

inertia, law of 141
    moment of 144
injury, ankle 158
    head 158
    impact 155
    knee 158
    leverage 155
    spinal 159
    wrist and forearm 158
input 150
interference, with skill learning 168

jonah back 186

kaboom 186
    front 94
kill 186
kip action 187
kipping 62
knee, drops 187
    injuries 158
knock out system 186
knowledge, of results 164, 166

landing platform 187
lateral axis 147, 148
law, of acceleration 144
    of inertia 141
    of reaction or counterforce 141
layout 187
lean 187
leaning 20
    rotation by 146
learning curves 166
leg braces 13, 14
legs, stiff 17
leverage injuries 155
lift 187
linear momentum 147
log roll 187
longitudinal axis 146, 148
lost 187

mat, throw in 188
miller 187
moment of inertia 144
momentum, angular 144
motivation 165
mount 187
multiple somersaults 107
    with twists, fliffes 117

nose bleed 158

one and one quarter front somersault tucked 48
one and three quarter front somersault, in the
    rig 80
    piked 108
    tucked 107
open 187
out bounce 187
overload injuries 155
overthrow 187

pads 13
personal factors of pupil 166
phasing 17, 163
physical dangers, of failure 172
pick-up 187
pike 187
pit tramp 187
porpoise 187
practice 166
    massed 167
    mental 167
    pressure 167
    spaced 167
    verbal 167
puck 187
pullover 187

radius, of gyration 144
randolf 103, 187
    ball out 187
randy 187
reaction, law of 168
retention of skill 168
rig 60, 187
rob roy 187
role, of pupil 171
roller 187
    stands 188
rotation, about the lateral axis 20
    about the longitudinal axis 20
    from the front landing position (cody kick) 83
routine 188
routines, examples of 178–84
    graded 177
    learning of 178
rudi 101
    ball out 92
    in 188
    out 188
rudolf 188

safety, code 13
    decks 13

side 188
scoop 18
seat drop 24
  full twist to seat drop 26
  half twist to feet, full twist to feet 25
sex 161
side 188
  somersault 55
stress, signs of 174
  affecting the coach 173
  effects of 171
  factors 172
  mild physical 174
  physiological 174
  severe physical 174
skill, analysis 168, 169
  learning 164
  subdivision of 167
  teaching 160
slide out 188
somersaults from the feet with twists 96
sommy 188
sports injury 155
spotter 188
spotters 59
springs 13
stand in 188
straight jump, with full twist 23
  with half twist 22
success 165
summation of forces 162, 163
suspension 14
support methods 57
swingtime 16, 188
swivel hips 26, 188
synchro 188

take off 17, 18, 19, 20
tariff 188
  system 175
tariffing principles 175
  examples 175–6
teacher 15, 165, 169, 170

three-quarter back somersault 82
  support 73
torque 143
tramp 188
trampoline, folding and unfolding 14
  safety 150
  terminology 185–8
transfer, of angular momentum 149
  of training 168
travel 188
triffus 139, 188
triple 188
  back somersault tucked 115
  front somersault with half twist out, tucked
    (triffus) 139
  full 188
  twisting back somersault 106
two and three quarter front somersault tucked 113
tuck 188
tucked, jump 21
  one and one quarter back somersault to back
    drop 54
turnover 188
turntable 32, 188
twister 188
twisting belt 188

unfolding 14

velocity 143
visual, aids 164
  contact 16
  illusions 152

warm up, aim of 153
  general principles 153
  physiological effects of 153
  psychological effects of 153
wear 14
webbing 15
weight 14
wrap 188
wrist injury 158